DISCOVER THE AMAZON

THE WORLD'S LARGEST RAINFOREST

—DISCOVER YOUR WORLD—
EXPLORE COOL SCIENCE | AMAZING HISTORY
20 ACTIVITIES

Lauri Berkenkamp

Illustrated by Blair Shedd

Nomad Press
A division of Nomad Communications
10 9 8 7 6 5 4 3 2 1
ISBN: 978-1-9346702-7-9

Illustrations by Blair Shedd; photograph on page 16 courtesy of NASA

Questions regarding the ordering of this book should be addressed to
Independent Publishers Group
814 N. Franklin St.
Chicago, IL 60610
www.ipgbook.com

Nomad Press
2456 Christian St.
White River Junction, VT 05001

green press
INITIATIVE

Nomad Press is committed to preserving ancient forests and natural resources. We elected to print *Discover the Amazon: The World's Largest Rainforest* on 4,315 lb. of Rolland Enviro100 Print instead of virgin fibres paper. This reduces an ecological footprint of:

Tree(s): 37
Solid waste: 1,057kg
Water: 100,004L
Suspended particles in the water: 6.7kg
Air emissions: 2,321kg
Natural gas: 151m3

It's the equivalent of:
Tree(s): 0.8 American football field(s)
Water: a shower of 4.6 day(s)
Air emissions: emissions of 0.5 car(s) per year

Nomad Press made this paper choice because our printer, Transcontinental, is a member of Green Press Initiative, a nonprofit program dedicated to supporting authors, publishers, and suppliers in their efforts to reduce their use of fiber obtained from endangered forests.

For more information, visit www.greenpressinitiative.org

FSC
Recycled
Supporting responsible
use of forest resources

Cert no. SW-COC-000952
www.fsc.org
© 1996 Forest Stewardship Council

COMING IN MARCH 2009
DISCOVER YOUR WORLD SERIES

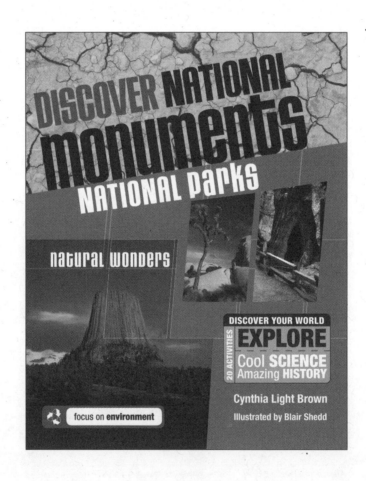

CONTENTS

INTRODUCTION

Amazonia: The Last Wilderness

There are few places left in the world where rivers are still unexplored. Where tribes of people live cut off from all contact with the outside world. Where there are thousands of plants and animals that most humans have never seen. **Amazonia** is just such a place.

Amazonia sweeps over a huge area of South America. It covers almost half of the continent, and is home to the largest **rainforest** on the planet. But it's more than just a rainforest. Amazonia also contains other **ecosystems**, including flooded forests, **savannah**, seasonal forests, and mangrove swamps. It touches nine different countries and is home to millions and millions of plants and animals. And the life-line of it all is the mighty Amazon River: the longest and largest river in the world.

This book takes you right into the world of Amazonia. Investigate the immense Amazon River, from its beginnings as a tiny trickle of melting snow in the Andes Mountains of Peru to its enormous mouth at the Atlantic Ocean on the coast of Brazil. Explore the layers of the Amazon rainforest, from the forest floor to the top of the canopy, and learn about the plants, animals, and people who live there. You'll learn how to make your way through the jungle without a compass or a map, find shelter and create fire, and gather food and use the natural world for all of your supplies. Along the way you'll discover how to avoid being bit, stung, poisoned, or eaten by predators both large and small.

Each section of this book covers a different topic. You can read the book straight through or skip around to uncover the information you find most interesting. The first section, **What Is the Amazon?**, explains all about Amazonia: the amazing Amazon River, the enormous rainforest, and the people who have lived there for thousands of years. If you just want to get going and do some exploring, turn to **Finding Your Way in the Rainforest** or **Finding Your Way by Water**. These sections will help you figure out how to set a course in the rainforest and follow it without getting turned around. You'll learn how to estimate your distance, mark a trail, build a raft, cross a river, escape from quicksand, and stay safe from water-based predators. See some of the amazing animals that live in Amazonia's vast water systems, such as the Amazonian giant river otter and the gorgeous, pink boto, the Amazon freshwater dolphin.

In **Finding Food**, you'll learn what plants and animals are safe to eat. Discover how to find them, and how to hunt and fish like Native Amazonians. In **Finding Water**, learn how to find fresh water from many different sources and make it safe to drink.

What about when the sun goes down? If you've always wondered how people stay overnight in the rainforest, go to **Night in the Amazon**. This chapter will help you decide what kind of shelter is best, and how to make it. You'll also learn how to build a fire without matches, and stay safe from night-prowling creatures both large and small.

Throughout the book you'll find fascinating facts and sidebars about some of the most incredible plants, animals, birds, and people of the rainforest. How about meeting the deadly bushmaster snake and the giant Amazonian leech? There are Try This! ideas throughout the book that you can do anywhere—you don't have to be in the Amazon. Activities range from learning to decipher animal tracks and make a simple fishing spear to building a gear raft or figuring out how much water you need to drink each day.

The Amazon is one of the largest and most important ecosystems on the planet. But it is threatened every day by human activity. Read this book to learn why—then find out how you can help save the Amazon rainforest.

Ready to discover the Amazon? Let's get going!

WORDS TO KNOW

Amazonia: a huge area surrounding the Amazon River in northern South America.

rainforest: a forest in a hot climate that gets a lot of rain every year, so the plants are very green and grow like crazy.

ecosystem: a community of animals and plants existing and interacting together.

savannah: a large grassy area with few trees.

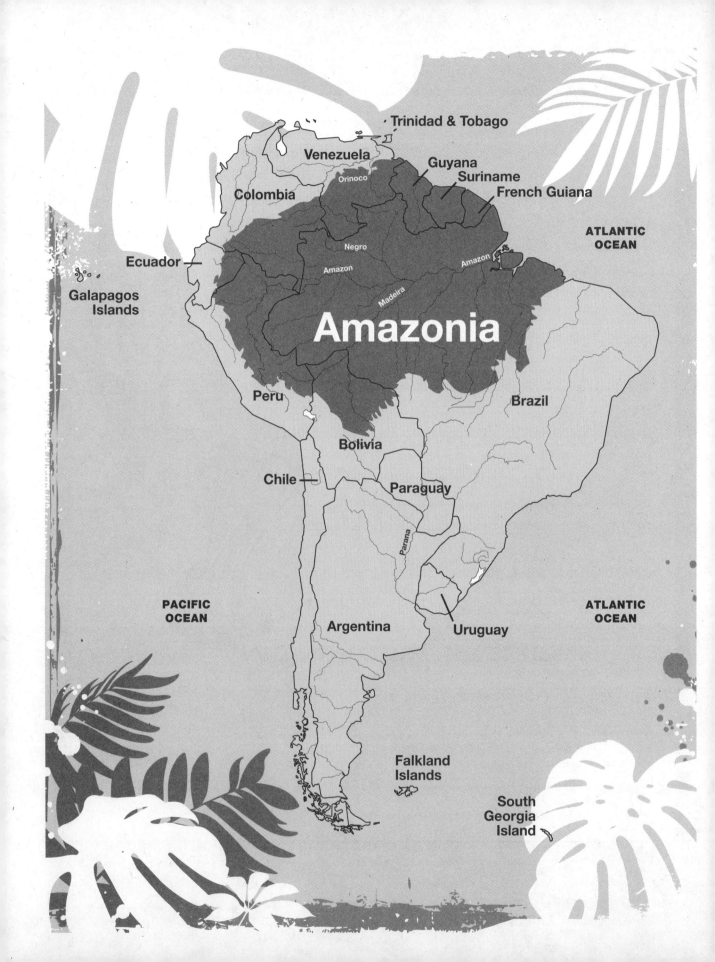

CHAPTER 1

What Is the Amazon?

Being in the rainforest is like being in a giant green tunnel. Trees and plants grow so thick that you can't even see the sky. The air is hot and **humid**. You're covered in sweat. All of a sudden it starts pouring and the rain comes down so hard, it feels like someone turned a faucet on over your head. Just as suddenly the rain stops. And the noise! You hear strange buzzing, chirping, squeaking, ticking, and squawking sounds all around you. Welcome to Amazonia, the largest rainforest on Earth.

Amazonia is what people call the enormous, saucer-shaped area of **tropical** rainforest and grassy savannah that covers much of the northern part of South America. This area is also known as the Amazon rainforest, the Amazon River basin, or just the Amazon.

Why Is It Called the Amazon?

The Amazon River got its name from a Spanish explorer of Ecuador and Peru named Francisco de Orellana. In 1541, Orellana sailed down the entire length of a huge river to the open ocean. Along the way, he and his men were attacked by what he thought were women warriors holding enormous weapons. Orellana fought back and escaped. When he reached safety, Orellana named the river after the **Amazons**, a race of women warriors from Greek mythology.

Amazonia covers about 3.1 million square miles (about 8 million square kilometers). If you could pick it up and move it northward, it would almost cover the entire United States! Amazonia touches nine different countries, but more than half of it—60 percent, in fact—is in the country of Brazil. So why is this huge area called Amazonia and not Braziliana? Because of the incredible waterway that makes this enormous rainforest possible—the Amazon River.

THE MIGHTY AMAZON RIVER

The Amazon River is big. How big? Here are some facts about the Amazon River that are pretty amazing:

- The Amazon is the longest river in the world—4,250 miles (6,840 kilometers) long. It begins flowing near the Pacific Ocean, then continues all the way across the continent of South America, and finally empties out into the Atlantic Ocean.
- The Amazon is also the widest river in the world. In fact, the mouth of the Amazon River is 200 miles (322 kilometers) wide, and even 1,000 miles (1,610 kilometers) upstream the Amazon is still 7 miles (11 kilometers) wide. That's almost too wide to see the other shore. And that's 1,000 miles inland!
- The Amazon is so deep that large ships can easily travel more than 2,300 miles (3,700 kilometers) up the river and still have hundreds of feet of space underneath their hulls. That's like traveling up a river almost the whole way across the United States on a cruise ship!

- The Amazon accounts for one-fifth of the world's water that flows from rivers into oceans.
- The Amazon pours 8 trillion (that's 8,000,000,000,000!) gallons of freshwater into the Atlantic Ocean every single day. That's so much water that even if you were to sail 100 miles (161 kilometers) out into the ocean, you'd still find freshwater, not salt water.
- The Amazon carries so much water that it would fill up Lake Ontario, one of the largest lakes in North America, in only three hours!
- The Amazon has more than 1,000 **tributaries**, 17 of which are also more than 1,000 miles (1,610 kilometers) long. These tributaries are some of the world's longest rivers, too.
- The Amazon carries so much **silt** that it formed the world's largest freshwater island, Majaro Island, in the middle of its mouth (where the river flows into the ocean). Majaro Island is the size of Switzerland!

That's not too bad for a river that starts as a five-inch stream in the **Andes Mountains**. The Amazon's source is a trickle of water flowing off the side of Mt. Mismi, an 18,363-foot-high (5,597-meter) mountain in southern Peru. That trickle flows into a slightly bigger stream, and then another. Those streams turn into rivers, which wind their way across the continent of South America. They are full of water from melting snow pack in the mountains and lots and lots of rain. From the western edges of Peru to the eastern edge of Brazil, more than 1,000 of these rivers and streams meet and grow and head down into the saucer of the Amazon River basin, until finally the Rio Solimões flowing west meets the Rio Negro flowing south, and they turn into the Rio Amazonas, the Amazon River.

WORDS TO KNOW

humid: a high level of moisture in the air.

tropical: a hot climate, usually near the equator.

Amazons: a nation of fierce, women warriors in Greek mythology.

tributary: a river or stream that flows into a larger lake or river.

silt: soil made up of fine bits of rock. This soil is often left on land when floods recede.

Andes Mountains: one of the longest and highest mountain ranges in the world. The Andes run 4,500 miles (7,242 kilometers) along the west coast of South America.

THE RIVER OF ARGUMENTS

There used to be two big arguments about the Amazon River. One was about where the river began. Another was about how long it was.

Scientists knew that the Amazon River started somewhere in the mountains of Peru, but where exactly? The definition of a river's source is the point that is the farthest away from the river's mouth. It also has to have water flowing into the river all year round. Finally, in 2000, scientists from five different countries on a National Geographic Society expedition traced the river's source to Mt. Mismi.

This discovery helped settle the other big argument—about the river's length. For many years, people argued about which river was longer: the Nile River in Egypt or the Amazon. The Nile measures 4,160 miles (6,695 kilometers) long while the Amazon was thought to be 4,020 miles (6,470 kilometers) long. But in 2006 when scientists measured the entire Amazon from its source on Mt. Mismi, they added 200 miles (322 kilometers) to its length. Now the Amazon is officially 4,250 miles long—64 miles (104 kilometers) longer than the Nile!

—FASCINATING FACT—

No bridges cross the Amazon River at any point.

Someone Actually Swam Down the Amazon!

Most people take a boat down the Amazon River, but on April 7, 2007, Martin Strel did something no one has ever done before: he swam 3,272 miles (5,268 kilometers) down the Amazon River. He did it in only 66 days!

Martin swam from Atalaya, Peru, to Belem, Brazil. He swam about 50 miles (80 kilometers) a day in all kinds of weather. Even when he was feeling sick. People worried that he would be attacked by sharks or piranhas, but his biggest problem was sunburn! Within two days of starting, his face and forehead were so sunburned that Martin had to wear a special mask. With this swim down the Amazon River, Martin broke his own Guinness Book World Record for long-distance swimming.

THE WORLD'S LARGEST RAINFOREST

There's one thing no one argues about. It's that the Amazon River supports the largest and most **diverse** tropical rainforest on the planet. Amazonia is home to so many different kinds of plants and animals that scientists can't count them all. Many **species** haven't even been discovered or named yet. Almost a third of all the world's living species of plants and animals live in Amazonia. Many of them live nowhere else on Earth.

Jaguar

How did this rainforest get so big and so diverse? There are two main reasons. The first is geography.

Millions of years ago, South America was part of a super continent called Gondwanaland. Gondwanaland also included Africa, Antarctica, and Australia. When Gondwanaland broke up, South America drifted on its own as a giant island. Many plants and animals that died out elsewhere—like sloths and anteaters—survived in South America.

Then a few million years ago, North and South America joined together. Plants and animals began moving back and forth between the two continents, making Amazonia even more diverse. For example, big cats like the jaguar originally lived only in North America. Over time, they moved south. Today, South America is the main **habitat** of the jaguar.

WORDS TO KNOW

diverse: lots of different species.

species: a group of plants or animals that are closely related and look the same.

habitat: an area where a species or groups of different animals and plants live.

ice ages: periods in time when the earth cools down and ice spreads over a large part of the planet.

The other reason why Amazonia is so big and diverse is because much of its climate has remained pretty much the same for a very, very long time. In other parts of the world, **ice ages** wiped out many species. But parts of the Amazon's rainforest stayed the same—hot, humid, and rainy for millions of years. Other parts of the rainforest changed a lot. The pockets of rainforest with a steady climate helped the old species of plants and animals thrive for millions of years, while the changing climate of other parts of Amazonia introduced lots of new species.

Anteater

Layers of the Rainforest

The Amazon rainforest has four layers: the emergent layer, canopy layer, understory layer, and the forest floor. Each layer is its own little **microhabitat**. Many plants and animals can only be found in one particular layer. Here is what each layer is like:

Emergent layer: This is where the tallest trees pop out, or emerge, above the rest of the rainforest. Some of these trees are more than 200 feet (61 meters) tall and their trunks can be as big as 16 feet (5 meters) around.

Trees in the emergent layer get plenty of sunlight, but they also are exposed to more wind and lots of rain. Plants that grow at the top of the emergent layer are usually small air plants called **epiphytes**. They get their nutrition from air, rain, and floating dust. Lots of birds, bats, insects, butterflies, and even monkeys live in the emergent layer. These creatures are safe up here, far above the predators below.

Canopy layer: Just below the emergent layer, the canopy layer creates a roof 60 to 90 feet (18 to 27 meters) above the ground. The canopy blocks out a lot of light from the forest floor, but it also prevents the soil from washing away when it rains.

Almost 90 percent of the animal species that live in the rainforest live in the canopy layer, including most bird species. There are also lots of monkeys, sloths, snakes, frogs, insects, lizards, and other animals living here. Many of these creatures never touch the forest floor.

The canopy layer is where most of the food of the rainforest grows, such as nuts and fruits. Vines called **lianas** grow here. These twine their way up the trees and tangle themselves in the top branches. There are also lots of **bromeliads**, **orchids**, and epiphytes in the canopy. These provide homes and food to lots of small creatures.

— FASCINATING FACT —

There are more than 1,500 different bird species in the Amazon rainforest. Many of them can only be found in certain types of trees in small areas of the rainforest.

Understory layer: This is the layer of the rainforest between the canopy and the forest floor. There's not much light here. Plants in this layer are usually less than 12 feet tall. The understory layer is home to most of the land animals of the rainforest, such as jaguars, anteaters, frogs, and snakes. It's also home to millions of insects.

Forest floor: The forest floor is dark and damp. Almost no sunlight reaches the forest floor, so things **decay** really quickly. Very few plants grow here. The forest floor is where you'll find **fungus**, **lichen**, and moss. You'll also find creatures that help the decaying process, like worms, millipedes, and ants.

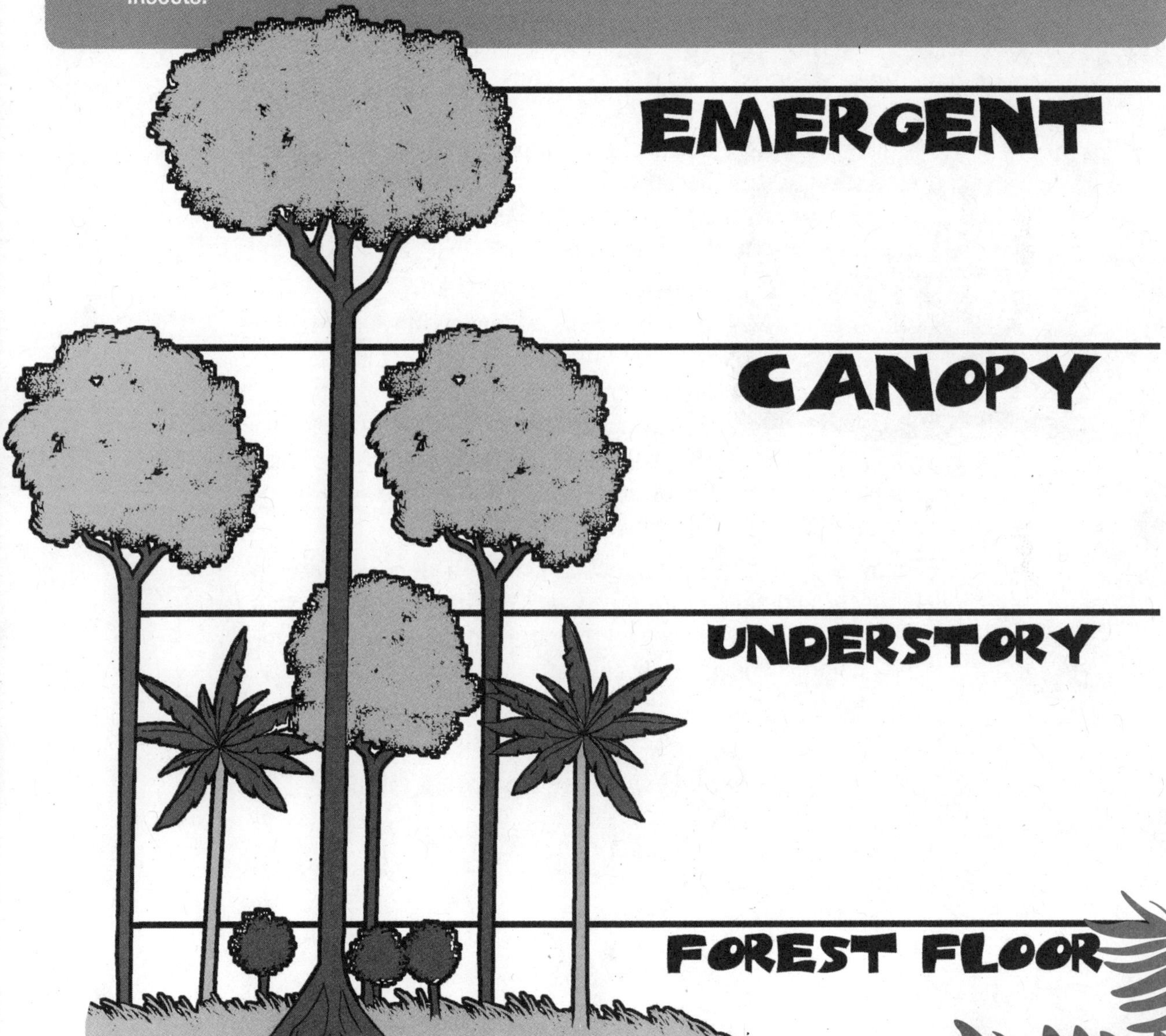

EMERGENT

CANOPY

UNDERSTORY

FOREST FLOOR

Studying the Canopy is Tricky!

Scientists need to study the canopy layer because that's where most of the plants and animals live. But it's not so easy when your laboratory is 90 feet (27 meters) in the air.

Over the years, scientists have tried lots of different ways to study the canopy layer. Some shot long ropes up into the trees. Some climbed up using mountain-climbing gear (this worked well but was dangerous). One scientist even tried to train a monkey to bring back samples of plants growing in the canopy.

Today, scientists use construction cranes, canopy walkways, ultralight gliders, and even balloons to observe the canopy. But we still don't know very much about what happens in the rainforest canopy, or even how many plants and animals live there.

— FASCINATING FACT —

Scientists have discovered a species of ant living in the Amazon that has existed for 120 million years!

WORDS TO KNOW

microhabitat: a very small, specialized habitat. This can even be a clump of grass or a space between rocks.

epiphytes: plants that grow on other plants. They get their food and water from the air and rain.

lianas: long, woody vines found in the Amazon and other areas of the world as well.

bromeliads: a tropical plant family that includes the pineapple.

orchids: rare and beautiful flowers.

decay: the process of rotting or deteriorating.

fungus: a plant-like organism without leaves or flowers that grows on other plants or decaying material. Examples are mold, mildew, and mushrooms.

lichen: a plant-like organism made of algae and fungus that grows on solid surfaces such as rocks or trees.

PEOPLE OF THE RAINFOREST

You might not see other people when you walk though the rainforest, but it's possible that other people can see you!

These people are Native Amazonians. They've lived here for thousands of years, mostly along the rivers. Most tribes have at least some contact with the outside world, but some tribes are completely isolated. They live by themselves in the rainforest, hunting, farming, and fishing, exactly the way their ancestors did thousands of years ago. The National Indian Foundation (FUNAI) is an organization set up to protect the rights of Native Amazonians. This group believes that there are more than 50 tribes that have absolutely no contact with the outside world.

Why do these tribes want to be left alone? Think about it: Before the first Europeans came to the Amazon in 1492, there were almost 6 million Native Amazonians in Brazil alone. Then the Europeans came and treated them terribly. They used the Amazonians as slaves, murdered them, and infected them with diseases that killed millions.

FASCINATING FACT

The Amazon used to flow in the opposite direction that it does today. Millions of years ago, the Amazon flowed from the Atlantic to the Pacific Ocean—east to west. When the Andes Mountains formed on the west side of the continent, the river was cut off from the Pacific and began flowing from west to east.

By the 1950s, only 100,000 Native Amazonians were left. To protect them, Brazil created places in the rainforest that were off limits to outsiders. The Native Amazonians live in peace there. Today, the population of Native Amazonians has grown to about 350,000 people. Most of them live in Brazil.

But even now, people illegally go onto native lands to hunt animals, search for gold, and steal oil and wood. The results can sometimes be deadly—usually for the native people.

Brazil's Rubber Boom

A hundred years ago, the only source of rubber in the world was found in Brazil, where rubber trees grow wild. If you cut into a rubber tree's bark, a liquid called latex oozes out. People collected the latex in buckets and then shipped it all over the world to be made into rubber.

Growing industries were desperate for more rubber. They couldn't get enough. This set off a rubber boom in Brazil. People raced to Brazil and stole land that belonged to the Amazonians. They enslaved the natives, killing them if they didn't produce enough latex, or if they tried to escape. Millions of Native Amazonians died during the rubber boom.

CHAPTER 2

Finding Your Way in the Rainforest

The vegetation in the rainforest is so dense and tall that it can seem impossible to find your way around. But even without a map or a compass, you can navigate the rainforest. You just need to know some simple strategies.

In 1971, 17-year-old Juliana Koepke was in a plane with 92 other people on board, flying over the tropical rainforest of Peru. The plane went through a freak thunderstorm and was struck by lightning. The last thing Juliana remembered was looking out the plane's window. The wing was on fire.

When Juliana woke up, she was still strapped to her plane seat. She had survived a plane crash that had killed everyone else on board. But Juliana was sitting on the ground in the middle of the Amazon rainforest. Alone.

Juliana remembered advice her father had given her. Water runs downhill. Water leads to people. So Juliana headed downhill. She found a stream and spent more than a week splashing her way **downstream**. She had to fight off clouds of mosquitoes, egg-laying flies, and clinging **leeches**. Juliana could hear planes above, searching for her, but she had no way to signal them. So she kept walking.

On the tenth day, Juliana found a hunter's hut. No one was there, but the hut had salt and kerosene in it. Juliana used the kerosene to kill worms that had **infested** her skin. The next day hunters arrived at the hut and took Juliana back to civilization. She had survived for 11 days on her own in the Amazon wilderness.

FASCINATING FACT

Amazonia touches nine countries:
Peru, Bolivia, Colombia, Ecuador, Venezuela,
Guyana, Suriname, French Guiana, and Brazil.

HEAD DOWNHILL

The Amazon River **watershed** is shaped like an enormous saucer. More than 1,000 rivers and tributaries flow from all directions into the Amazon River itself. Most people in Amazonia live on or near these rivers. If you can make it to a river and follow it downstream long enough, you'll find people.

The most important thing to remember in the Amazon is to stay alert. Since the Amazon rainforest has the greatest diversity of plants and animals on Earth, you are likely to meet up with lots of different kinds of creatures. All have forms of protection from **predators**. You may not think you're a predator, but other creatures will think you are if you surprise them.

Amazon River Delta

Bamboo

When you're traveling in the Amazon you have to watch where you step. Dangers include snakes, poisonous spiders, and even large, stinging ants. It's also important to carry a stick. Bamboo is easy to break into pieces and very light to carry. The flexible stalks of the pono palm also make a good walking stick.

Sweeping the stick in front of you will uncover dangers lurking in the deep underbrush. The swishing sound alerts animals that you're coming, so they can get out of the way.

HOW TO MOVE IN A STRAIGHT LINE

If you were trying to find your way in the rainforest it would be easy to walk around in circles without even knowing it. Moving in a straight line may seem easy, but it's almost impossible to do without visual cues. Why? Because people aren't **symmetrical**. One side of your body is stronger than the other.

WORDS TO KNOW

downstream: in the direction of a stream's current, away from its source.

leech: a wormlike animal found in water that latches on to another animal's skin and sucks its blood.

infest: to live in or on in great numbers as a parasite.

parasite: an animal or plant that lives on or in another plant or animal, feeding off of it, without any benefit to the host.

watershed: an area where all the water drains into one river or lake.

predator: an animal that eats other animals.

symmetrical: the same on both sides.

TRY THIS: FIND YOUR DOMINANT EYE

Find an object a few yards away. Put your finger out at arm's length so it's centered on the object. Close your left eye. If your finger stays on the object, you are left-eye dominant. If the object jumps to the right, you are right-eye dominant.

For example, you might not notice it, but one of your legs is slightly longer than the other. This means that you swerve in one direction when you walk. Another physical factor that affects your direction is eye dominance. You tend to veer towards whichever eye is stronger.

Many people also turn their head slightly to one side while walking. Again, you go in the direction your head is tilted. Even bad weather can affect your direction. People lean their heads away from bad weather, so their bodies follow.

TRY THIS: Discover Your Swerve Pattern

Walk blindfolded for about 30 steps on a beach, a snowy field, or a muddy yard with no obstacles. Then take off your blindfold. You'll be able to see which way you swerve by your footprints. You can also do this experiment in a wide hallway. Have a partner watch in which direction you veer as you walk blindfolded down the hall.

USE LANDMARKS TO STAY ON COURSE

The best way to stay on a straight course is to use **landmarks**. You use landmarks all the time. For example, you turn right at the traffic light and left at the gas station.

The problem in the Amazon rainforest is that the landmarks are plants and trees. They all look alike, which makes it very easy to get turned around. The solution is to walk in as straight a line as possible, and **blaze** your way as you travel. Marking your path means that you can trace your steps. If you were lost, it would help someone follow your path.

FASCINATING FACT

Many of the plants that grow in the rainforest, such as philodendrons, are plants you can grow inside your house. This is because the forest floor has such poor soil and gets so little light.

TRY THIS: cairns

Cairns are another good way to blaze trails. In a place with lots of rocks cairns are heaps of rocks or stones that help mark the trail. You usually find them at turns or places where paths meet or split apart. The rainforest does not have many rocks so cairns can be made out of sticks, or any other material that is handy, easily noticed, and that won't be destroyed by animals or bad weather.

Blazing a trail is easy. Simply line up two objects ahead of you at eye height, such as tree trunks or large vines. Try to place one object as directly in front of the other as possible. Then turn around and do the same thing behind you.

Now walk back and mark the objects behind you first. This is called "back marking." Back marking makes it easy for you to turn around and retrace your steps. It also gives you reference points when you are scouting landmarks in front of you.

As you walk forward, mark your landmarks well enough so that anyone walking the same path will notice them. Keep lining up new landmarks in front of you, while also checking the backmarked landmarks behind you. This will help keep you on a fairly straight path. It will also allow other people to follow your path.

Native Amazonians have their own methods of trailblazing. You probably wouldn't even notice them unless you looked very carefully. One method is called leaf doubling. Amazonians simply bend a leafy branch back onto itself so the undersides of the leaves are showing. The underside of the leaf is usually duller than the top side, and is very noticeable against the vivid green of the forest.

WORDS TO KNOW

landmark: a noticeable natural or man-made feature used for navigation.

blaze: to mark out a path or trail.

Beware of Snakes

Most movies that take place in the Amazon show the rainforest practically dripping with snakes waiting to attack at any moment. But the truth is most snakes that live here aren't poisonous or aggressive. In fact, they are pretty hard to spot at all if you don't know where to look. People usually come upon snakes by accident.

The most common snakes in the Amazon rainforest are non-poisonous constrictors. This family includes the boa constrictor. You've probably seen boas in pet stores, zoos, or maybe you even have your own boa as a pet. Boa constrictors are the second-largest snake in the Amazon. They can grow up to 16 feet long. They eat small birds, **mammals**, and other snakes.

Of course, there are also some very poisonous snakes in the Amazon. These are the cause of most of the snakebite deaths in South America. The largest family of poisonous snakes is the pit vipers. They hunt at night using heat sensors on their heads to feel the warmth of live **prey**.

The most common pit vipers in Amazonia are the jararaca, also known as the *fer-de-lance*. You can always recognize a pit viper by its triangular-shaped head and very large fangs. Most also have some kind of horseshoe-shaped pattern on their backs. Some species of jararaca live only on the forest floor, and some live only in the trees. Some even live in urban areas! More people get bit by jararacas than any other kind of poisonous snake.

By far the most feared snake in the Amazon is the rare and deadly bushmaster. Its Latin name is *Lachesis muta*, which means "silent decider of fate." This amazing pit viper is the most venomous snake in the entire **Western Hemisphere**. It can grow to 14 feet (4¼ meters) in length, and has fangs that are up to an inch long. Bushmasters are able to strike many times in just a few seconds, biting over and over again. They have a nasty reputation for being very aggressive. Snakebites from bushmasters result in death about 80 percent of the time.

Bushmasters live on the forest floor. They are stealth predators, which means they lie waiting for their prey to come to them. When their prey is within range, bushmasters strike from as far away as four feet. It's very unlikely that you'll run into a bushmaster, but if you do, you are more likely to step on it than anything else. Like all rainforest snakes, bushmasters are designed to blend in with their environment. And since most snakebites occur in the foot and lower leg, the best way to avoid being bitten by a bushmaster or any other snake in the rainforest is to watch your step.

TRY THIS: FIND THE SUN

Here's a way to find east or west in the rainforest, or in any forest, for that matter. Lie down in the shadow of a tree in either the early morning or late afternoon. Look up. The sun will cast a light on the tree's canopy. Part of the tree's canopy will be illuminated and part will be in shadow. In the morning, the part of the canopy that is lit with light will face east and in the afternoon and evening it will face west.

FINDING YOUR DIRECTION

The simplest way to figure out which direction you're going is to look at the sun. You see where it is in the sky, estimate the time of day, and find east or west. The problem with doing this in the rainforest is that you usually can't see the sun at all. The enormous tree canopy blocks it from view.

But there are ways to find your direction. Trees tend to sprout more new branches on the side facing east. So if you're walking through the rainforest, the side of the trees with more branches is probably east!

WORDS TO KNOW

mammals: a class of animals that includes humans. These animals have backbones, nourish their young with milk, and are mostly covered with hair.

prey: an animal hunted by a predator.

Western Hemisphere: the half of the earth that contains North and South America.

Boa Constrictor

— FASCINATING FACT —
Most people will make a full circle in about half an hour if they set out to walk in a straight line blindfolded.

TRY THIS: make a simple compass

You can make a simple, fairly accurate compass with just a magnet, sewing needle, cork, and saucer of water.

Take the magnet (a bar magnet works best but a refrigerator magnet will also work) and rub it in one direction along the needle. Do this about 10 times. This will magnetize the needle a bit. Now push the needle through the piece of cork so that both ends of the needle are sticking out. Then place the cork in a small saucer of water. The floating needle will point to magnetic north!

MARKING DISTANCE IN THE RAINFOREST

Scientists estimate that the average visibility in the rainforest is only about 150 feet (46 meters). Because everything is so green, it's very hard to gauge distance or direction. But determining how far you've gone can be very important.

Think about this story: a married couple set out from a ranger station and hiked for about an hour on a well-marked path. Then they decided to turn off and explore the forest. After walking a few hundred yards away from the path the woman fell and hurt her ankle. Her husband raced back to the path and ran to the ranger station.

Bullet Ants

Bullet ants looks like large, wingless wasps, and they are the insect with the most painful sting in the world. They're also known as "24-hour ants" because that's how long the pain from a sting lasts.

Bullet ants grow to be as large as an inch long. They are the largest ant in the Amazon, and one of the most common. They usually build their nests in and around the big roots of trees, and sometimes in holes in trees.

Bullet ants aren't aggressive. They only use their stingers for food gathering, or when their nest is attacked. Just before bullet ants get ready to sting they make a sound like "Eep eep eep" and they give off a musky smell. That's your cue to get out of there, fast!

Some native Amazonian tribes use the bullet ant as part of a ceremony welcoming young men into adulthood. For example, members of the *Sateré-Mawé* tribe of Brazil put dozens of bullet ants into a woven glove. The boys put on the glove and see how long they can stand to have their hands in it. The longer they keep the glove on, the more they prove their manhood.

——FASCINATING FACT——

Vines called "fire lianas" have chemicals in them that can burn your skin if you touch them. So remember to take a good look at the plants before you reach for them! You'll learn what to look for in Chapter 4, Finding Food.

It didn't take him long to get help, and he and the ranger ran back down the path right away. The problem was that the hiker didn't know exactly where his wife had fallen. It took a search party three weeks to find her. By then it was too late.

So how do people in the Amazon determine how far they've traveled, especially in the rainforest where landmarks are hard to find? A simple way is to count your steps. It takes most people about 2,000 steps to travel a mile. Most people can usually walk a mile at a good pace in about 20 minutes.

But to keep track of 2,000 steps can be confusing. One way to make this easier is to hold 10 pebbles in your right hand. Count just your right-foot steps. Each time you reach 100 right-foot steps, move one pebble from your right hand to your left hand. When your right hand is empty, you've walked a mile—and it probably took you about 20 minutes.

To keep track of how many miles you've walked, use a different set of markers. Move one of those markers from your right to left pocket every time you've gone five miles.

FASCINATING FACT

Just like animals, many trees and plants have ways to protect themselves from predators. Some of those defenses can hurt—a lot—if you touch them. For example, cecropia trees are known as "ant trees." That's because stinging *Azteca* ants live inside the hollow stems (trunks). When something touches the tree, thousands of ants feel the vibrations and swarm out to attack whatever has disturbed their home.

THE FINGER METHOD

It's also tricky to figure out distances *between* objects in the rainforest. This is because everything tends to be the same color and size, so your eyes can play some tricks on you. A good way to estimate how far you are from a certain object is to use the finger method. The finger method is based on the principle that the distance between your two eyes is about one-tenth of the distance from your eye to the end of your finger on an outstretched arm.

Sometimes TV Experts Aren't So Smart

One TV survival expert gave this advice: if you're lost in the rainforest, climb a tall tree to see where you are. The problem is that the tallest trees in the Amazon rainforest can be 250 feet (76 meters) tall. They have almost no branches below the canopy layer. Unless you have a jetpack, you aren't going to be able to climb a tree to look around.

Because there's so little sunlight in the rainforest, many plants grow tall very quickly—they're in a hurry to reach the sun! It's also why so many plants have enormous leaves. The bigger the leaf, the more area for light to hit. The more light, the more energy the plant can make to grow. Some plants have leaves that are more than a foot across.

Because the sunlight has to filter down through so many big leaves it makes the entire forest glow a vivid green. Explorers have said that walking in the rainforest is like moving through a green fishbowl.

Luckily, this filtered light also makes the forest floor pretty easy to walk on. Many movies show explorers hacking their way through the rainforest with machetes, but most places in the Amazon aren't like that. Not enough sunlight reaches down to the forest floor for big, thick plants to grow. Instead, the floor of a rainforest is usually bare, brown, and covered in roots and decomposing vegetation. You may trip over roots that are growing out of the ground, but it's pretty unlikely you'll have to hack your way through them.

First extend your arm in front of you and hold up your pointer finger. Line up your finger with the object using only one eye (it doesn't matter which one). Pretend that your finger is actually touching the object you're looking at. Don't move your finger, but now look at the object with the other eye. Try to figure out how many feet away from the object your finger moved. Multiply that number by ten. That's roughly how many feet you are away from the object.

Why Objects Look Closer or Farther Than They Are

Whenever you are trying to figure out how far away an object is, remember these simple rules.

Objects usually look closer than they are when:

- The object is up or downhill from you.
- The object is across water, snow, or sand.
- The object has a bright light shining on it.
- The air is clear.

Objects usually look farther away than they actually are when:

- The color of the background is the same as the object.
- The object blends into the background.
- You are looking at the object over uneven ground.
- The object is at the end of a tunnel or surrounded on two sides.

CHAPTER 3

Finding Your Way by Water

Rivers are the roads of the rainforest. There are more than one thousand rivers in the Amazon rainforest! Anyone venturing into the region will likely need to cross or travel on a river.

The best way to navigate an Amazonian river is to walk alongside it. There are often trails made by animals or people. Following these trails downstream for as long as possible, especially along a well-worn path, will bring you closer to people.

What if the trail ends or there is an obstacle.? You may need to cross the river, or even travel in the water to keep heading downstream. But what dangers lurk beneath the surface?

Rafting the Amazon

You'd think that lots of people would have traveled the entire length of the Amazon by boat. But, actually, only a few people have been able to do it successfully.

In August 1985, Polish kayaker Piotr Chmielinski was the first person to make it down the length of the Amazon under his own power. Chmielinski was part of an expedition that began in the mountains of Peru, at what was then thought to be the Amazon's source. Chmielinski did his whole journey in a **kayak**, reaching the mouth of the Amazon six months after he started.

HOW TO CROSS A RIVER

Crossing a river can be dangerous. All rivers have a current. The current can be barely noticeable, or it can be strong enough to pull you rapidly downstream. A river can get deep very quickly as you head toward the middle. Currents are always stronger in the middle of a river than at its edges. Here are some good rules to follow if you want to cross a river:

- **Do not go in if you can hear rushing water, or a roaring noise.** This means the current is very strong and there are rocks and other obstacles in the river. Try to go back **upstream** until you can find a place where the river is slower and shallower.

- **Pick a spot on the other bank where you'll land**. Do this before you get in the water. Always pick a spot downstream from you. It is easier to move with the current and cross at an angle instead of directly across the water. The place you pick should be easy to reach. Don't try to come out of the water where anything is over your head, slippery, or potentially dangerous such as rocks or overhanging branches. And remember: if you can't see the other side of the river, do not try to cross it. Walk downstream until the river narrows enough so that you can see what is on the other bank.

WORDS TO KNOW

kayak: a light, narrow canoe useful for traveling in fast currents.

upstream: against the direction of a stream's current, toward its source.

balsa: a tropical tree with very light wood that floats.

tannins: substances found in plants that are used to turn animal skins into leather.

- **Use a stick if the river is shallow enough to walk across.** Find a stick that is about as thick as your wrist and as high as your shoulder. Plant the stick upstream and use it as a support against the current while you walk across.

- **Use a balsa pole if the river is deep.** In the tropics, if the river is too deep to walk across and the current is slow, you can swim or float down the river using a balsa pole. **Balsa** is a tree that grows in the rainforest, often near riverbanks. It is very light and floats well. Balsa is easy to recognize: balsa trees are tall and straight, with grayish-beige bark that is smooth but tends to flake. Balsa leaves are large and heart shaped, and the leaves and branches bunch at the top of the tree. They are easy to cut down. Cut a balsa pole slightly shorter than you are and strip off any branches. Hold onto the balsa pole while floating on your back, feet first. This will make it easier for you to push off of any obstacles in the river, and let you see where you are going!

The Different Colored Rivers of the Amazon

There are three types of rivers in Amazonia: blackwater, whitewater, and clearwater. Blackwater rivers originate in the lowlands. They flow through swamps and flooded forests. They are full of acidic soil and sand, and are usually the color of dark tea. Their color comes from the **tannins** of decaying leaves and debris. Strangely enough, blackwater rivers have some of the purest water on Earth.

Whitewater rivers begin in the Andes Mountains. These mountains are young, tall, and crumbly. So rock, dirt, and minerals easily wash off them into whitewater rivers. Whitewater rivers have lots of plant and animal life, and are a creamy yellow color.

The clearwater rivers come from ancient parts of what is called the Brazilian and Guayana shield—earth that is low, old, and already very broken down. Not a lot of minerals or nutrients come into these rivers, and there is not a lot of plant life here.

Boto

Giant Otter

The Amazonian Giant River Otter

Imagine an otter the size of an adult man—6 feet (2 meters) long or more—and weighing up to 70 pounds (about 32 kilograms). This is the size of the giant river otter, the largest and most endangered species of otter in the world.

Giant river otters are known as the wolves of the river, because they hunt in packs and are fearless. They will take on prey much larger than they are, including giant anacondas and caimans. In fact, it is the otters' fearlessness that has helped make them so endangered. Instead of running away from hunters, giant river otters swim right up to the hunters' canoes to intimidate them. This makes them easy to kill. Giant river otters have velvety-soft fur, making their pelts very valuable.

Since the late 1980s it has been illegal to hunt the giant river otter, so the wolves of the river may make a comeback.

The Amazon's Pink Dolphin

The Amazon's flooded forests are home to one of the most amazing animals on earth—the Amazon River dolphin. Known as the *boto*, the Amazon River dolphin is a freshwater mammal that grows up to almost 9 feet (3 meters) in length, weighs 400 pounds (182 kilograms), and is bright pink!

People who live in Amazonia believe that when someone drowns in the river, their spirit enter the bodies of the botos. These dolphins are said to have magical powers. At night, the botos come to visit people in the shape of handsome young men. If you meet up with a mysterious, handsome stranger at night, beware—it could be a boto in disguise!

FLOODED FORESTS

Calm water is easier to cross than running water, but it also has hidden dangers. If you were crossing a calm bit of water in the Amazon, you might suddenly notice that there were lots of sticks and branches beneath you. You would probably think that these sticks and branches are from fallen trees, but they might be from something else. One of the most fascinating things about the Amazon are its flooded forests—you might be swimming above trees that are buried underwater!

During the rainy season—November to March—the rivers of the Amazon flood. When this happens, the waters often rise up to 50 feet (15 meters). Entire forests become submerged in water—sometimes for long periods of time. In some areas, forests can be covered by water for as long as 8 to 10 months of the year.

The trees and shrubs in these forests grow very quickly when the floodwaters go down. In fact, scientists recently learned that the Amazon rainforest actually grows more in the dry season than it does in the wet season. This is exactly the opposite of what happens elsewhere.

Flooded forests are the cafeterias of the rainforest. When the floodwaters rise over the land, they help add nutrients to the forest soils, lakes, and floodplains. Lots of fish and other creatures migrate to the flooded forests every year to find food and shelter in the treetops. In fact, many fish eat fruit from trees that in the dry season would be thirty feet above the ground! They swallow the fruit whole and pass along the seeds as they swim. The seeds then go elsewhere in the river, take root, and begin to grow into new fruit trees.

FASCINATING FACT

At the Meeting of the Waters in Manaus, Brazil, the Rio Negro (a blackwater river) and the Rio Solimões (a whitewater river) meet but don't mix for more than 50 miles (81 kilometers). Instead, the two rivers flow side by side, one dark brown, the other creamy yellow, until the dark waters are finally absorbed into the Amazon River.

Tambaqui

Other fish, such as the tambaqui, have very strong teeth good for cracking and eating fruits and seeds that fall from the tops of trees. The tambaqui wait under the trees for the fruit to ripen. When the fruit falls and hits the water, the fish feel the vibrations and come to the surface to eat.

MAKE A RAFT TO GROSS WIDE RIVERS

Sometimes a river or lake is just too wide to swim across. In order to cross, people in the Amazon have to build rafts. But what do they make them out of? How could you make a raft?

While balsa wood makes the best rafts, bamboo works well, too. People have used bamboo for centuries to make sturdy rafts for travelling on the rivers of Amazonia. Like balsa, bamboo is easy to find and it is light and strong, and floats well.

You need six stalks of bamboo about eight feet long. With a knife, notch out windows (holes through the bamboo) on opposite sides of the bamboo on both ends of the poles. Line up the windows of the poles so you can push another bamboo pole through, and lash the cross pole to the raft using flexible liana vines. If you want extra **buoyancy**, make a second layer of bamboo poles with one less pole so the bottom layer has six poles and the top layer has five. Lash the two layers together. Your raft will ride higher in the water.

The lianas—or any rope—you used to tie the raft together will fray pretty quickly when the raft is on the water. You would want plenty of extra liana coiled on the raft for repairs.

FASCINATING FACT
Trees in the flooded forests usually have bark that is covered in thick, cork-like tissue that protects it from the water. The tree's leaves are protected by a water-repellent covering.

Beware the Bees!

Believe it or not, in some parts of the Amazon the biggest danger isn't from big cats or snakes—it's from honeybees! While they normally won't bother people, they can be very aggressive if their nests are disturbed.

You can't outrun honeybees, but you can outswim them. If you disturb a honeybee nest and you are near water, the best thing to do is dive in and swim underwater as far as you can. Then try to come up under some vegetation, like tree branches. If you aren't near water, try to hide in the thickest brush you can, so the bees have a hard time flying in to sting you. The best way to avoid being attacked by a colony of honeybees is to follow the S's: move slowly, speak softly, and don't stink (they can smell you!).

THE DANGERS OF AMAZONIA'S CALM WATERS

Lots of creatures live in the mud and muck at the bottom of Amazonia's rivers and streams, including freshwater stingrays. Stingrays have a very sharp barbed tail that they whip up if they feel threatened. The stingray's barb carries a very painful poison. The poison isn't deadly, but it definitely hurts a lot!

Another animal found in the Amazon's rivers and streams is the electric eel. Despite its name, the electric eel isn't actually an eel at all. It's a freshwater fish that lives in slow-moving waters. The electric eel can grow as long as 8 feet (2$\frac{1}{2}$ meters). It kills its prey by shocking it with an electric charge. Some of the shocks are strong enough to kill a horse!

Another thing to watch out for in the Amazon is quicksand. Quicksand isn't actually sand, it is soil that has become so wet that it can't hold any weight. During the rainy season, the ground in Amazonia is wet almost everywhere, especially near lakeshores and riverbanks.

Quicksand isn't a bottomless pit, and you aren't going to drown in it—don't believe the movies! It's usually just a couple of feet of sticky, gooey, sucking mud or sand.

But it can still be tricky to get free from it. What usually happens to people when they step in quicksand is that one of their feet will sink first. Then they shift their weight onto the other foot to try to pull the first foot out, and end up with both feet stuck.

If you were ever to find yourself stuck in quicksand don't do this! Instead, you should fall forward onto the quicksand. This distributes your weight more evenly over a larger surface. Then slowly pull your whole body forward so your feet come free. Don't stand up and have the same thing happen all over again. To keep moving through quicksand, stay low and crawl through it.

TRY THIS: BUILD A RAFT

The easiest raft to build is a one-person seat raft. You can build a seat raft out of wood that floats well. Or if you just want to have fun, use a foam noodle. Cut the noodle in half so you have two equal lengths. Tie the noodles together at both ends with rope. Leave enough space between the noodles so you can sit in between them with one noodle under your knees and the other noodle behind your back. The seat raft will keep you above the water and let you guide yourself with your legs.

The Scary Candiru

A fish that frightens people even more than the piranha is the tiny candiru. These small river catfish are also called toothpick fish because they are so thin. Candirus are almost impossible to see because they are transparent. There are only a few rivers in the Amazon that contain candiru. The candiru is a parasite, which means it lives in or on another animal and feeds off it. For example, candiru will swim into the gills of fish when the fish exhales. The candiru attaches itself to the inside of the fish and sucks its blood.

So why would a little fish like the candiru frighten people? Because people say that candiru are attracted to human urine and will swim up your urine stream and lodge itself inside your body. So if you have to go to the bathroom, don't do it in a river in Amazonia!

AMAZONIA'S CALM WATER PREDATORS

WORDS TO KNOW

buoyancy: the force that makes something able to float.

anaconda: large constrictor of tropical South America, usually found living in swamps or slow-moving water.

Among the animals that live in the slow, stagnant waters of Amazonia's lakes and swamps are some of the most fascinating and rare creatures on Earth. They can also be very dangerous. But most of them view you as the predator, not the other way around.

Anaconda: The **anaconda** is the world's biggest snake. It isn't the longest—that honor goes to the Asiatic reticulated python—but the anaconda can grow to almost 30 feet (9 meters) long and can weigh up to 550 pounds (250 kilograms). This makes it the world's most massive snake.

The anaconda preys on animals such as fish, capybaras, tapirs, caimans, deer, and even jaguars. Anacondas are slow-moving predators that hunt by stealth. They can stay underwater for 10 minutes at a time, waiting for their victim to come close enough to attack. The anaconda bites its prey and holds the animal in its jaws until it can coil itself completely around the body and squeeze it to death. Then the snake swallows the animal whole.

It is pretty unlikely that you'll run across an anaconda in the Amazon, though. They are very wary of humans. Unless they are actively hunting, anacondas will avoid any confrontation. You may be lucky enough to see an anaconda sunning itself in tree branches or lying on the bank of a shallow, slow-moving river.

Caiman: Caimans are part of the alligator family. They are the largest freshwater-based predator in the Amazon River basin. There are many different species of caiman, ranging from the dwarf caiman, which grows to about 4.5 feet, to the enormous black man, which can grow as long as 20 feet (6 meters). Caimans usually live near riverbanks, where they build large, mounded nests in which they lay up to 40 eggs during the dry season

Caimans are night hunters. They eat fish and larger animals that go in or near the water, such as capybara, other mammals, and sometimes even humans. The safest way to deal with caimans is to avoid them altogether. Only go in calm water during the day.

─FASCINATING FACT─
Caimans have extremely strong jaw muscles for clamping down. But the muscles for opening up their mouths are quite weak. You can easily hold the jaws of a caiman together using only your hands.

WORDS TO KNOW

caiman: a reptile that's very similar to an alligator. It lives in Central and South America.

manatee: a large, plant-eating mammal that lives and swims in the Amazon and other parts of the world, including India and Florida.

stillwater lake: a lake within the boundaries of a wetland, often surrounded by swamp-like plants and habitat.

wetland: a low-lying area that is filled with water.

Piranha: The piranha is the Amazon's most famous fish. They are carnivorous, which means they eat meat. Piranhas are attracted to thrashing movements and the smell of blood. They attack their prey with fierce, sharp nips. Their razor-sharp teeth can gouge out chunks of flesh from their victims. The blood from these cuts attracts more piranhas, and they can have what is called a feeding frenzy, snapping at everything around them. People have seen a school of piranhas in a feeding frenzy strip a large animal down to its skeleton in less than 15 minutes.

Piranhas have a scary reputation from the movies, but the truth is that they usually don't attack humans. However, if food is scarce and you happen to be bleeding, piranhas will bite first and ask questions later.

——FASCINATING FACT——

Predators such as caimans and piranhas view lots of splashing and noise as signs of an injured animal. Injured animals usually make easy hunting. So if you swim, do it slowly and calmly. Don't splash or make a lot of noise, and definitely don't go in the water if you are bleeding.

The Marvelous Manatee

One of the most amazing animals in the rainforest is the Amazonian **manatee**. It is the largest mammal found in the waters of the Amazon River basin. The Amazonian manatee can grow as long as 9 feet (3 meters) and weigh as much as half a ton. This is 1,000 pounds (454 kilograms)! However, it is still the smallest species of manatee.

All manatees are vegetarians. During the wet season, these gentle creatures eat water hyacinth and water lettuces that grow in and around the **stillwater lakes** of the **wetlands**. In the dry season, they head to deep river channels where they live together in groups of up to eight manatees. There has been a hunting ban on manatees since 1973. But river dams make it hard for manatees to migrate. These dams have seriously reduced the numbers of manatees living in the Amazon today.

CHAPTER 4

Finding Food

There are a lot of challenges to survival in the rainforest, but at least you shouldn't starve to death. Food is everywhere. You just need to know where to look for it.

Back in 1914, Theodore Roosevelt—who had been America's president from 1901 to 1909—was a member of an expedition exploring the Amazon. They didn't pack many food supplies because they thought there would be plenty of wild animals they could hunt. They were wrong.

Members of the expedition found almost no large animals, and the ones they did spot were hard to hunt. They were surrounded by millions of acres of edible plants, insects, and other creatures. But they didn't know it.

WORDS TO KNOW

malnourished: when you don't get enough of the right food to keep you healthy and strong.

lush: word to describe lots of richly green plants.

nutrients: the substances in food and soil that keep animals and plants healthy and growing.

hectare: a metric unit of land equal to 107,000 square feet, or about 2½ acres.

The explorers ate only the tops of palms, Brazil nuts, and the few small animals they could shoot and kill. By the time the expedition reached civilization, all of the men were sick and **malnourished**. Some were close to death.

Palms

The Amazon rainforest is a plant paradise. Plants grow everywhere. They twine all over each other. They bloom like crazy and grow giant leaves. What causes this super-charged growth, this amazing **lushness**? The rainforest has absolutely ideal growing conditions for plants: warm temperatures, plenty of rain, and lots of sun. Those conditions make organic matter such as leaf litter, old trees, and dead animals decompose very fast—10 times faster than they'd decompose in a temperate forest like those found in much of the United States. So a dead leaf that would take almost a year to decompose in a northern forest takes only a month in the Amazon. All the **nutrients** that come from decomposing plants and animals get sucked right back up into the plant roots, making them grow like crazy.

The amazing rate of growth also helps to explain why trees and plants of the same type are often spaced far apart in the rainforest. In many places, there will be will be lots of different kinds of trees in an area, but not very many of each kind. In fact, one biologist working in the Amazon rainforest in Peru counted 300 different species of trees in one **hectare** (10,000 square meters or about 2½ acres).

Because they grow so quickly, trees in the rainforest tend to have pretty shallow roots. So trees often fall over. When a large tree falls over in the rainforest, it creates a break in the canopy. Lots of light floods in. The first kinds of plants and trees to grow back in a newly opened area are always light-loving plants and trees. Scientists call these nomads or pioneers.

Rainforest Farming

Native Amazonian tribes know how to farm *and* keep the rainforest healthy. They do this by growing lots of different crops in and around existing rainforest plants. For example, the gardens of the Tirio tribe of Guyana look like a small hole in the jungle where one large tree has fallen over. But these small garden spaces fill in quickly with fast-growing plants that attract birds and game animals, so the Tirio can both grow crops and hunt in their gardens.

These gardens may look messy, but the Tirio know exactly where each plant is. And they have a good reason for planting each plant there. For example, they will plant manioc very close together to form a natural roof so other plants don't get too much sun. The Tirio will also plant many different kinds of the same crop in an area. This way, if an insect or disease destroys one type of plant, the others are safe.

WORDS TO KNOW

minerals: nutrients found in rocks and soil that keep plants and animals healthy and growing.

Sahara Desert: the world's largest desert, located in northern Africa.

atmosphere: the air or gas surrounding a planet.

Northern Hemisphere: the half of the earth that is north of the equator. This includes North America, Europe, Asia, the Middle East, and Northern Africa.

FASCINATING FACT

The Amazon rainforest is fertilized every year from 50 million tons of **mineral**-rich dust that comes from an unlikely place: the **Sahara Desert**. Every year, dust from a very small area of the desert, called the Bodele Depression, is blown up into the **atmosphere** and across the Atlantic Ocean by the **Northern Hemisphere's** winter winds and lands in the Amazon rainforest, bringing important mineral nutrients to keep the rainforest healthy and growing. Amazing!

Nomads sprout, grow, and produce seeds very quickly. But since nomad species love lots of light, their seedlings can't thrive in the same area as the parent tree. Why? Because there isn't enough light once the nomad tree has grown tall and produced shade. So nomad species (also called pioneers) almost always have tricky ways of **propagating** their seeds. Most nomad species have fruit or seeds that are very attractive to birds. The birds eat the fruit or seeds, fly away, and then spread the seeds along the way. New nomads grow in other parts of the rainforest, and the process repeats itself.

WORDS TO KNOW

propagate: create new plants.
alkaloids: natural chemicals found in plants. Nicotine is an alkaloid.

FINDING EDIBLE PLANTS IN THE AMAZON

The tricky part about finding food in the rainforest is figuring out what is safe to eat and what isn't. Many plants in the Amazon have chemicals called **alkaloids** in them. Alkaloids help protect the plants from predators. Many of those alkaloids can also help cure lots of diseases. That's something that the native people of the Amazon have known for centuries.

The problem is that some plant alkaloids are also poisonous to humans. Cashew nuts, for example, are a common snack food all over the world—after they have been roasted, that is. In their natural state, cashews are closely related to poison ivy and poison oak. The nut has a really irritating, poisonous oil that has to be roasted away so the fruit can be eaten. Guava, papaya, and Brazil nuts are common foods in the rainforest. In fact, there are lots of other plants that are safe to eat too. But if you were ever lost in the Amazon, you wouldn't want to try a new food without doing a safety test. A safety test can take a lot of time, but it is important to avoid poisoning yourself. So how would you test the plants of the Amazon?

— **FASCINATING FACT** —
The Amazon rainforest grows most during the dry season.

First, you would want to check over the plant. If it has **mildew** on it, or if it smells strongly bitter or just plain bad, don't eat it. Mildew is a fungus that can be very poisonous. Strong smells help a plant keep away predators, and can often be a sign that the plant is **toxic**. Plants with milky white sap are often toxic, too. You should also not eat plants that have pods full of beans or seeds.

When you finally find a plant that looks and smells good, you want to separate it into different parts: stems, leaves, flowers, and fruit. Each of these parts should be tested separately as follows. First, rub a little of one part on the inside of your elbow. Wait to see if your skin reacts to the plant. If you don't have a skin reaction after about 15 minutes, touch a little of the plant to your lip. If it stings, burns, numbs your lip, or makes you have any kind of reaction, don't go any farther. If not, put a small piece on your tongue, and hold it there for about 15 minutes. Don't chew it and don't swallow. If you have no reaction after 15 minutes, chew and swallow. And then wait. If you have no reaction after several hours, you can be pretty sure that the part of the plant you've tested is safe to eat.

Keep in mind that you have to test each part of the plant for safety. Just because the stem is safe doesn't mean the

TRY THIS: Search for tropical fruit

You don't need to be in the rainforest to eat food that grows there. The next time you are in the grocery store or fruit market, look for cashews, Brazil nuts, passion fruit, guava, papaya, avocadoes, mangos, acai, or cupuacu. All of these fruits come from the Amazon.

leaves are also safe. Even plants in North America have edible parts and poisonous parts. For example, rhubarb is a common garden plant that people use to make pies and jams. Rhubarb stalks are delicious, but its leaves are poisonous. So out in the wilderness you need to take the time to test each part of the plant before you eat it.

Something else to keep in mind in the rainforest is that a lot of plants look alike: Very green and leafy. So make sure the plant you want to eat is the same one you tested before. But if you've taken the time to test a plant, chances are you are very familiar with it!

AMAZON'S ANIMALS

Even though Amazonia is a huge place, you won't find giant herds of roaming animals like in Africa. There just isn't enough of the same kind of food to eat in one place for herds. Instead, the rainforest is home to lots of different animals that live alone. Most of them eat plants, fruits, and nuts.

The few animals that are **carnivorous** are spread out. For example, the largest cat, the jaguar, has a hunting territory of up to 60 square miles. Jaguars need that much space to find enough animals to survive.

WORDS TO KNOW

mildew: a fungus that often looks white and can be found on rotting food and plants.

toxic: poisonous.

carnivorous: a plant or animal that eats meat. Some plants trap and digest small animals, mostly insects.

forage: search for food.

If you went to the Amazon, you may never even get to see the largest animals of the rainforest, such as the tapir, giant anteater, or jaguar. Some are so endangered that they are rarely seen, and all of them are quite cautious. They will sense you (by sight or smell) before you see them and will usually stay as far away from you as possible.

There are a few animals in the Amazon that don't live alone. One of these is the peccary. Peccaries look like wild pigs, and live in herds. As many as 50 roam through the rainforest together, digging for roots and **foraging** for fruit. One explorer described the noise of a herd of peccaries as a rumbling, clacking roar.

Peccary

Peccaries love fruit—and following peccary tracks will often lead to the base of a fruit tree. Peccaries also happen to be one of the jaguar's favorite foods.

Howler monkeys also travel in packs. They are called "howler" monkeys because of their well-known call. It sounds almost like a mule braying, although some think it sounds more like a lion roaring. They can be heard up to 3 miles (5 kilometers) away. If you hear a lot of roaring in the night, don't panic. It is probably just a howler monkey.

Howler Monkey

WORDS TO KNOW

medicinal: having properties that can be used to treat illness.

property: a quality or feature of something; the way something is.

shaman: a native person with the power to heal.

quinine: a bitter-tasting drug made from cinchona tree bark that is used to treat malaria.

malaria: a blood disease caused by parasites often found in jungle and rainforest environments. It is spread by mosquitoes.

salicylic acid: an acid from a willow tree that is used to make aspirin.

Amazon Plants That Are Medicines

Native Amazonians know a lot about the chemical and **medicinal properties** of plants. Scientists have even traveled to the Amazon to train as assistants to tribal medicine men, or **shamans**.

The Amazon rainforest has already given the world two very important natural medicines that have changed our lives. **Quinine** helps prevent **malaria**, and **salicylic acid** is the main ingredient of aspirin. Many more natural remedies are being studied and tested for their use against deadly diseases such as HIV and AIDS.

FASCINATING FACT

Amazonia is home to the largest eagle, snake, anteater, armadillo, spider, freshwater turtle, freshwater fish, rodent, otter, and toad in the entire world.

Brazil Nuts

Brazil nuts grow inside a wooden shell that looks a bit like a coconut. Brazil nut trees can be 90 feet (27 meters) tall, and can produce 1,100 pounds (500 kilograms) of Brazil nuts during each harvest. Harvest is during the rainy season, and it can be dangerous work. This is because the heavy wooden shells full of Brazil nuts can drop off the tops of the tree and hit someone's head far below.

After the shells have fallen, workers gather them from the ground and chop off the top. They shake out the Brazil nuts, rinse them in a nearby stream, dry them, and ship them off. Brazil nuts are full of oil, which people use for cooking and to burn for light. Some native tribes use the wooden shell as a container for their arrow poison.

WORDS TO KNOW

palm: a tropical tree with fronds.
lowlands: land that is lower and flatter than surrounding lands.

Palm Plants That Are Safe to Eat

Many different types of **palm** trees have hearts that are edible. The palm heart is about 3 feet (1 meter) below where the palm leaves sprout. It is very crunchy and tastes a bit like celery. To get to the palm heart, you have to cut down the whole palm tree. Native Amazonians often use all the different parts of the tree after cutting it down.

Astrocaryum palms are tall palm trees with rings of really sharp spines around their trunks. They are easy to spot, and live all over the **lowlands** of the Amazon rainforest. Native Amazonians use the astrocaryum palm for everything from food to shelter. They make hammocks, baskets, and rope from the leaf fibers, and eat and drink the fruit and oil.

Another palm tree that has an edible heart and very good fruit is the peach palm. These trees grow in clusters of trunks, and their leaves have enormous sharp spikes—up to 5 inches (about 10 centimeters) long. Their fruit grows in bunches. They are orange-red on the outside and yellow inside, with a hard seed in the middle. Despite its name, peach palm fruits aren't sweet. They are more like potatoes. Amazonians boil this fruit in salty water and mash it up.

HUNTING GAME

Hunting animals in the rainforest takes patience and skill. Many Amazon tribes use rifles to hunt game these days, but some tribes still use the same weapons their ancestors did. The Matses tribe of Peru uses bows with arrows that are more than 6 feet long. They make their arrows from cane they grow themselves. Then they stick on bamboo arrowheads with **resin** and beeswax. Finally, they attach bird feathers from curassows, eagles, condors, and macaws so the arrows will fly in a straight line.

Some Amazonian tribes tip their hunting arrows with poison called **curare** to kill larger game. The poison usually comes from a mixture of certain rainforest plants. Each tribe has its own secret method of making curare.

Other Amazonian tribes use blowguns. The Matis tribe of Brazil uses blowguns that are almost 13 feet (4 meters) long. All blowguns shoot poison-tipped darts. The natives coat the ends of the darts with curare, then blow the darts out of the blowgun toward their prey.

Using a blowgun takes great skill. To hunt monkeys, for example, the hunter must climb into the trees, sight his blowgun, take aim, and shoot. The poison works slowly, so the hunter usually has to climb down the tree and chase the animal through the woods until it dies. Often the monkey will die and stay in the tree. It's much easier to just point a rifle up and shoot a monkey, even if it scares off the rest of the monkeys. This is why many Native Amazonians have given up on the old ways of hunting and now use rifles.

— FASCINATING FACT —

Native hunters who use blowguns are incredibly accurate. Some can hit a target as tiny as a hummingbird from 150 feet (46 meters) away!

Palm Grub Farms

The Yanomamo tribe of northern Brazil actually farms palm grubs. Grubs are soft, wormlike larva of beetles. The Yanomamo cut down palm trees, remove the palm hearts, then let the trunks rot for a few months. Beetles lay their eggs, which hatch into grubs. One rotted tree can hold up to three or four pounds of grubs. Some of the grubs can be as big as a mouse! The Yanomamo eat grubs raw, or they wrap them in small leaf packages and stick them in hot coals to roast.

Most people would find it almost impossible to hunt game in the rainforest, but there's plenty to catch and eat. In fact, there's more walking, crawling, and flying food here than any place else on Earth. For example, insects are incredibly nutritious, easy to catch, and simple to eat. They have more protein than beef. You just have to eat a lot of them to fill your stomach.

Worms are also high in protein. Just dig them up, rinse or brush them off, and squeeze them to get rid of any worm poop inside. You can eat them raw or dry them in the sun and eat them like worm jerky. Another insect that is easy to find and even considered a delicacy by many Amazonians is the palm grub. They check palm trees rotting on the ground by putting their ears to the trunk. If there are palm grubs in the trunk you can hear them moving inside. They are 5 inches (13 centimeters) long, fat, and white with a black head. The Native Amazonians slit them open up the back, snap off the black head, and suck out the insides. Or perhaps you'd prefer to roast them over a fire. Roasted grubs are supposed to taste like bacon.

WORDS TO KNOW

resin: a substance from plants that is sticky like glue.

curare: poison made from plant or animal venom, used for hunting.

Poison Dart Frogs

Poison dart frogs are one of the most colorful animals in the rainforest. Their bright coloring is a signal to predators to stay away. Poison dart frogs can be black and green, red and blue, black and blue, or even bright yellow. All are highly poisonous. In fact, their poison is the most powerful poison in the world!

Lots of frogs secrete mild poison through their skins so predators such as hawks and snakes won't eat them. But the poison secreted by poison dart frogs will kill predators that swallow or even lick them. Red and blue poison dart frogs are the least deadly, but their poison is still so powerful that only 2 micrograms of it could kill a human—and each frog contains about 200 micrograms. This powerful poison is produced from the food the frogs eat. For example, there are chemicals in certain kinds of ants that turn into poison in the frog's body. If the frog stops eating that type of ant, they are no longer poisonous. This is why some people can keep poison dart frogs as pets.

TRY THIS: make an insect meal

Most insects are fine to eat, but some are tastier than others. Follow these guidelines to eat a delicious insect dinner:

- Don't eat insects that have a bad smell or give you a rash if you hold or handle them.

- Take off the legs and wings of large insects before you eat them because these parts can scratch your mouth and throat.

- Avoid insects with bright colors. Colors are a warning to predators. That means you, too.

- Cook beetles, grasshoppers, and other insects with hard outer shells. They often carry parasites.

- Don't eat caterpillars with hairs on them. The hairs are barbed and can irritate your throat, and some caterpillar hairs store venom.

FISHING FOR SURVIVAL

Much of Amazonia is covered in water. The many rivers and lakes of the rainforest are home to more than 3,000 different species of fish. Fishing provides Amazonians with plenty of food all year long. There are two main ways to fish in the Amazon. One is with a fishing line and a hook. The other is with a spear.

You can make your own fishing gear. A fishhook can be made out of wood, bone, thorns, or any combination of these things. Because there are so many kinds of thorns in the Amazon, a thorn hook would be the easiest to make. First you would get three or four thorns. Then take a piece of palm or vine fiber, wind it around the top of the thorns to bind them together, pull as tightly as possible, and tie it off. It should look a little bit like a tiny ship's anchor.

Another piece of palm or vine fiber tied to the thorns makes a good line. You may need to tie several pieces of fiber together to make the line long enough to fish.

For bait, use grubs, worms, or any slow-moving insect you can stick on the hook. You will have the best luck catching a larger fish if you get a small minnow to use as bait. Remember that a thorn hook is going to be pretty delicate, since it's tied together. You will probably have to make a bunch of these before you get one that holds up to a strong tug by a fish.

You can also try spearing fish. Often it is hard to see fish swimming beneath you because they blend in so well with the river bottom. If you have a white or light-colored shirt, you can take it off and anchor it on the bottom of the riverbed with stones. When a fish passes over the shirt it's easier to spot.

FASCINATING FACT

There are so many different insects in the Amazon rainforest that scientists can't even begin to count them all. They estimate, though, that there are more than 30 million different types.

Remember that when light passes through water, it bends. This is because water is a different density then air. So when you look at a fish underwater, the fish isn't exactly where you see it. Even if you look straight down at the fish you are trying to spear, it will look bigger and closer to the surface than it actually is. If you are looking at the fish from an angle, such as behind or in front, aim your spear behind and below where you think the fish is swimming. You'll have a better chance of spearing it.

Spearing fish takes practice. You need to get the hang of estimating the difference between where the fish looks like it is swimming and where it actually is.

TRY THIS: make a fishing spear and fish weir

Making a double-pronged spear is actually pretty easy. Find a long, straight **sapling**. Split one end of the sapling about 6 inches (15 centimeters) down the middle. Then push a small wood chip down into the split to spread apart the two halves of the sapling. Sharpen those two ends into points.

If you are near a shallow river with a quick current, you can make a simple fish trap, or weir, to catch small fish. A fish weir is a wall that directs fish in one direction, and a pen to keep the fish from leaving once they've been trapped.

You can make a simple weir by arranging river rocks to form a C, with the opening of the C facing the shore. Then make a wall of rocks leading to the opening of the C, **perpendicular** to the shore. This will cause fish swimming downstream or upstream to move into the opening of the C. Fish aren't that smart, and will have a hard time figuring out how to get out of the C. You can then try to hook the fish or spear the fish.

WORDS TO KNOW

sapling: a young tree.

perpendicular: when an object forms a right angle with another object.

insecticide: a chemical that kills insects.

organs: things like the heart, lungs, stomach, and liver.

Fishing with Nature's Insecticide

Rotenone is a chemical found in many tropical plants and trees. We use it in **insecticides**, but many Amazonian Indian tribes use rotenone to catch fish. First, they crush up the plants or trees into a pulpy paste. Then they put the paste in the water. The rotenone in the paste prevents the fish from taking oxygen from the water through their gills, so they float to the surface. The Indians can then spear the fish or shoot them with bows and arrows.

FASCINATING FISH

The Amazon has more fish species than any other body of water on Earth, including the Atlantic Ocean. Many of the fish in the Amazon have adapted to their environment in strange ways. The leaf fish, for example, looks and acts like a dead leaf. It lives near the sides of river banks and lakes, blending in with the dead leaves and branches that collect near the sides. The leaf fish even has a lower jaw that sticks out like a leaf stem. When it is disturbed, it doesn't swim away. Instead, it floats gently to the bottom of the river to safety until the danger is past, then drifts back to where it was—just like a leaf.

The four-eyed fish looks like it can walk on water. The fish really has only two eyes, but each eye is divided in half horizontally. The fish lies just under the surface of the water, and can see both above and below the water surface equally well. If it senses danger, it moves its fins so fast that it actually skips across the surface of the water as it swims to safety.

Leaf Fish

TRY THIS: CLEAN AND COOK A FISH

Once you've caught your fish, whack it hard on the head to kill it. Cut off the fins. You can also cut off the head, but it is easier to cook over a fire if you leave the head on. Cut along the bottom of the fish from just behind its head all the way to the tail. Stick your hand inside and pull out all the **organs**. Rinse the fish to clean out any leftover stuff inside. You could eat the fish raw if you don't have a fire, or you can push a stick through the fish's mouth and hold it over the fire and cook it until the flesh turns white.

CHAPTER 5

Finding Water

It may seem odd to have to worry about finding drinking water in the Amazon rainforest. After all, it gets about 80 inches of rain every year—that's about 6$\frac{1}{2}$ feet (2 meters)! The problem is that the air is so hot and humid that your body has to work very hard to cool down. That's why it's so important to drink lots in this climate.

If you don't replace the water that you lose in sweat, you become **dehydrated**. Besides being thirsty, you might also feel dizzy, really tired, or get a headache. Your mouth might get dry and sticky. You might stop urinating, or your urine might turn really dark. All of these are signs that you are dehydrated. The solution is to drink more water. But where can you find water?

While it's true that there are lots of rivers and lakes in Amazonia, finding water that is safe to drink can be tricky. Why? Because animals, insects, and microscopic creatures use the same water sources that you use. Take the tank bromeliad, for example. Tank bromeliads are a kind of plant that grows attached to the sides of trees. They look a bit like the tops of pineapples and have an indentation that makes a shallow bowl in the middle of their leaves. That bowl is constantly filled with rainwater—and life. Each tank bromeliad is home to a whole little ecosystem: mosquito larvae, tadpoles, algae, salamanders, dragonfly larvae, frogs, and even snakes. In fact, in one study in the Costa Rican rainforest, scientists counted more than 250 species living in one type of tank bromeliad! Those 250 species are only a tiny fraction of the number of creatures that share the water of the rainforest with you.

WATER-BORNE DISEASES

When you're in the rainforest, you need to be careful what you drink and where you get it. Disease spreads easily in water. When sick animals and people go to the bathroom near water sources, they often **contaminate** the water with **bacteria** and tiny parasites. If you drink contaminated water in the rainforest, you can get very sick. You can even get sick from swimming in it. There are some pretty nasty diseases you can get from parasites in the rainforest water. They range from disgusting to deadly.

WORDS TO KNOW

dehydrated: suffering from a great loss of water in the body.

contaminate: to pollute or make dirty, so the water isn't healthy to drink.

bacteria: microorganisms found in soil, water, plants, and animals that are sometimes harmful.

For example, a lot of people get diarrhea from contaminated water. It is usually caused by bacteria or single-celled parasites called amoebas. The amoebas live inside a person's large intestine and can stay there for a long time without making the person sick. Sometimes, though, the amoebas attach themselves to the lining of the small intestine, and that causes trouble.

Other water-borne diseases are deadly. One of the most interesting—and unpleasant—is called schistomiasis, or snail fever. Freshwater snails carry a microscopic worm that gets into freshwater pools and ponds in the rainforest. If you drink this water or swim in it, the worms can get into your body. They go right to your liver, where they lay thousands of eggs. Ick. The good news is that schistomiasis is treatable, and when caught early, completely curable.

TRY THIS: Determine How Much Water You Need Per Day

You'd be surprised how much water your body needs each day to stay healthy. While most people say you need to drink eight 8-ounce glasses of water—that's almost 2 liters—it's just an average. The more you weigh, the more water you need.

Here's a way to figure out exactly how much water *you* need. First, find out how much you weigh in pounds. Then divide that by two. That number is how many ounces of water your body needs each day. To figure out about how many glasses of water that is, take the number of ounces and divide that by 8. If you drink soda, sugared drinks, or drinks with caffeine, you need to add an extra glass of water.

Is it more or less than you thought?

The Giant Amazonian Leech

Here's another reason not to drink directly from a water source—you may encounter a giant Amazonian leech. It's the world's largest leech, and can grow to be more than a foot ($1/3$ meter) long and almost 4 inches (10 centimeters) wide! Giant Amazonian leeches are found in marshes and **stagnant** water ponds through the Amazon rainforest. They attach themselves to animals and suck their blood.

Young giant Amazonian leeches usually attack small **amphibians**. Adults will attach themselves to larger animals such as cattle, capybaras, caimans, and even anacondas.

WORDS TO KNOW

stagnant: very still, not moving.

amphibians: animals like frogs, toads, and salamanders. The young have gills like fish but adults breathe air.

immunity: when a person has been exposed to a disease before and can resist it.

Native Amazonians Wiped Out By Disease

When the first Europeans came to the Amazon centuries ago, they brought diseases with them that were new to the Native Amazonians. These diseases included the flu, measles, pneumonia, and tuberculosis. Unfortunately, the Amazonians had no **immunities** against these common diseases. Hundreds of thousands of them died.

Today, native tribes still catch diseases that are brought from the outside. A few years ago, tribes of Native Amazonians in northwestern Brazil were given water-purifying filters and information written in the most common native languages about how to protect themselves from water-borne diseases, especially those that cause diarrhea in children.

THE SAFEST WATER SOURCES

So where can you find safe water? Your best bet is in streams and rivers where the water is moving quickly. Fast-moving water means danger to animals, so they avoid it. Streams or rivers with thick brush growing right up to the edges tend to be safer too. The brush makes it harder for animals to go to the bathroom in the water. If you find lots of animal tracks near water that's a good sign not to drink it. The water in the middle of a stream where the water is moving more quickly, will always be safer than the water at the shore.

Plants can also be a safe source of water. Another name for the water liana is the "aqua vida" (life-giving water) vine. The vine can be several inches thick and has a gray, scaly bark. It contains a lot of drinkable water. To get the water, you need to cut the vine in two places.

First, cut the vine off as high as you can reach. Keep the cut-off part upright. Then cut off the vine about a foot from the ground. Hold that end upright, too. The water that is stored in the vine will come out the bottom and is safe to drink. When the water starts to dwindle, make another cut about six inches from the top. That should start more water running again. You can do this as many times as the length of your vine allows.

TRY THIS: QUICK WATER SAFETY TEST

You can try a simple test to see if water is contaminated. Just pour some very fine sand into a bowl of water. If the sand falls quickly to the bottom, it means that the water is relatively clean. If the sand floats, there is something in the water making it more dense than it should be.

Parrot

There are lots of lianas and vines in the rainforest. If you cut a vine and sticky or milky sap runs out, don't drink it. Milky, white, or strong-smelling sap can be poisonous. Before you drink any water from plants in the rainforest, do a quick safety test. Just put a few drops of the liquid in your hand and touch the drops with your tongue. If it burns or affects you in any way, don't drink it. If it doesn't bother you, it should be okay to drink.

Another plant that often has water in it is bamboo. You can shake bamboo to hear if there is water in its joints—it will make a sloshing sound. Break open the joints and pour the water into your container. You can also cut off the top of a bamboo plant, bend it over, and tie it to the ground. Water will drip out of it over time.

Banana plants contain water in their trunks. First, you need to cut off the banana plant about a foot above the ground. Then scoop out the trunk to form a bowl. Over time the trunk will fill with water. It will be really bitter at first, but if you toss out that water the banana trunk will eventually fill with drinkable water. A banana plant can supply you with fresh water for several days once the bitter water is gone.

Amazing Amazonian Parrots

When you find water, you're also likely to find birds. The Amazon has some of the most amazing and colorful birds in the world—and lots of them! Scientists have counted more than 1,500 different species of birds in Amazonia. In one study, scientists counted 500 different kinds of birds in only a few square miles of rainforest.

Most birds live in the canopy layer, which makes bird watching tricky. But the most famous birds in Amazonia are also the most visible—parrots! There are 20 different species of parrots. They range from large, very brightly colored macaws to tiny parrotlets, which are the size of sparrows.

Parrots travel together in flocks. They often gather on tree branches at open riverbanks and marshes. Hundreds, and even thousands of parrots, especially macaws, can gather at a single site.

STAGNANT WATER SOURCES

If the only water available is still water, such as in swamps, ponds, or even a deep puddle, you can drink from it if you absolutely need to. But first you should try to make the water cleaner. The best thing is to put iodine tablets in the water and then boil it. If you don't have iodine or a fire, you can filter the water using a few simple methods.

If the soil is sandy or muddy, dig a hole about 12 inches (¹/₃ meter) deep a foot away from the main water source. The water will filter up through the bottom of the hole after about half an hour. Since the water has traveled through the sand or dirt, some of its impurities have been filtered out. It's probably safe to drink now.

You can also use your shirt to make a simple filter. First soak your shirt in the water, then wring it out into a container. Filtering the water through your shirt will not get rid of everything, but it will remove some of the organisms and debris that could be in the water.

Of course if you were really desperate for water, you'd be better off drinking *any* kind of water than no water at all. In 1999, Colin Angus and two friends decided to hike through the Peruvian mountains down into the rainforest. They didn't realize they'd have to hike through a desert, and they quickly ran out of water. The men were so dehydrated they thought they might die.

Then they stumbled across a small pond that was used by hundreds of birds. The pond's water was bright green, covered in algae, and its edges were chock full of bird feathers, poop, and other debris. The men knew they could get really sick drinking this water, but the alternative was to have no water at all. They used their shirts as filters and drank as much of the repulsive water as they could. That water ended up saving their lives, and they were able to continue on their journey to safety.

Watch What You Drink!

You should never drink directly from a water source. Instead, take the water from the source and pour it into another container before you drink it. Otherwise, you could be like the unlucky English explorer who lay down on the riverbank, stuck his face in the water—and got the tip of his nose nipped off by a waiting piranha!

Another reason you should pour water into another container is to make sure you aren't swallowing anything bad. A story went around in the early 1970s about a child in Brazil who drank directly from a bamboo water pipe at a resort. He immediately had terrible stomach pains. No one could figure out what was wrong with him, and the child died. Doctors found a tiny snake in his stomach. They concluded that the snake had been in the bamboo water pipe and the child had swallowed it without realizing it. The snake had bitten the child in the stomach and killed him.

FASCINATING FACT

When you're in the jungle you lose up to 25 percent of your body fluid every day.

CHAPTER 6

Night in the Amazon

The rainforest during the day can be beautiful and exciting. The rainforest at night can be scary—and sometimes dangerous. So you need to find a shelter. You can either build a shelter or you can use natural shelters such as fallen trees or rocks. Maybe you can even find an existing shelter that has been abandoned. But to spend the night in the rainforest you need some kind of protection from the weather and predators, both large and small.

Night comes to the rainforest quickly. The Amazon rainforest is close to the equator, so the sun sets almost perpendicular to the earth. Instead of a long, lingering twilight like you might be used to, night falls like a curtain being dropped over a window. Moonlight doesn't even begin to penetrate the thick canopy overhead. So it gets really dark.

WORDS TO KNOW

nocturnal: nocturnal animals are active at night.
diurnal: diurnal animals are active during the day.

It also gets really loud. More than half of the animals in the rainforest are **nocturnal**. This means they are more active at night than during the day. Many of these animals would be eaten by **diurnal** predators, which are predators that are active during the day. So many animals wait until the safety of night to come out to hunt, mate, and socialize. And for nocturnal predators, animals that wouldn't be available to hunt during the day are active and plentiful at night.

These creatures let you know they are there! From the constant noise of frogs and insects to the incredibly loud cries and calls of howler monkeys and other large animals, the nighttime sounds of the rainforest can take some getting used to.

Cane Toad

Amazonian Frogs

The most ear-splitting noise in the rainforest at night comes from the thousands of frogs that live there. Almost three-quarters of the frogs in the Amazon rainforest are nocturnal. Most of these frogs don't live in water. They don't need to. The rainforest has such high humidity that the damp air keeps the frogs' skin safely wet all the time. There are more species of frogs in the Amazon (over 300) than any other kind of amphibian. And more are being discovered every year!

Each species of frog has a different sound to attract mates. They have calls that sound like whistles, chirps, grunts, and shrieks. The cane toad makes a call like a low rumble. The boatman frog makes a call that sounds like someone is tapping oars on the side of a canoe. The most famous Amazonian frog, the poison dart frog, isn't nocturnal. It is only active during the day.

DANGEROUS NOCTURNAL PREDATORS

Most of the animals in the rainforest are not a threat to humans. In fact, most are not even **carnivores** (meat eaters). And the animals that are either carnivores or **omnivores** (they eat both plants and animals) usually eat much smaller prey than you. They like to eat insects, frogs, fish, birds, and very small mammals. But there are some nocturnal animals that are very dangerous, even though you are unlikely to meet them.

Jaguars: The largest land predator in the Amazon rainforest is the jaguar. It can grow to 6 feet (2 meters) long and weigh up to 360 pounds. Jaguars live and hunt alone, usually at night. They attack their prey by pouncing on the animal's back and breaking its neck or crushing its skull with a single, huge bite. The jaguar's name, in fact, comes from the native Amazonian word, "yaguar," which means, "he who kills at one leap." Jaguars hunt all sorts of smaller animals, including tapirs, deer, peccaries, caimans, sloths, turtles, fish, and giant otters.

The jaguar is **revered** by many rainforest tribes. In fact, members of the Matis tribe of Brazil use body decorations and **tattoos** to look like jaguars. When they turn 15, Matis men and women are tattooed on their cheeks with stripes to mimic the whiskers of the jaguar. The ceremony is an important mark of adulthood in Matis culture, and the ceremony takes up to two weeks.

Jaguars have been so overhunted for their fur that they are considered a vulnerable species. In 1973, laws were passed that made trading in jaguar skins illegal. You will probably never see a jaguar in the rainforest, but you might come across jaguar tracks near freshwater sources. A jaguar's tracks, like all cat tracks, have four toes and a center pad. The front foot track looks quite round, while the back track often looks longer than it is wide.

While it's unlikely that you'll run into a jaguar, it's not impossible.

Think about what happened to Yossi Ghinsberg. Yossi was on a rafting adventure with a friend when his raft overturned and the two were separated. Yossi struggled for three weeks in the rainforest on his own with little in the way of gear or supplies.

One night, Yossi couldn't find shelter before the sun went down, so he cleared away some brush, strung a mosquito net between a few trees, and lay on the ground. In the middle of the night he heard a rustling near his net. He turned on his flashlight, and saw a jaguar only a few feet away. Yossi yelled and threw sticks but the big cat didn't move. He finally took a lighter and his can of bug spray and lit a spray of insect repellent towards the jaguar. The flash blinded Yossi for a few moments. When he regained his sight, the jaguar was gone. But there were paw prints only a foot away from Yossi's head.

Vampire Bats: Depending on where you are in the Amazon, you might run into a predator from a horror movie—the vampire bat. Out of the 950 different kinds of bats in Amazonia, the vampire bats found there are the only true vampire bats in the world. They survive entirely by drinking blood from mammals—including humans. They use their razor-sharp teeth to scoop out a tiny bit of flesh, and then lap up the blood that starts flowing. A chemical in the vampire bat's saliva keeps the blood from clotting. Vampire bats won't suck all the blood out of you, but they can be deadly because they might carry **rabies**. In fact, a few years ago, 14 people in a small town on the Acuti-Pereira River in Brazil died from rabies after being bitten by local vampire bats over a period of two nights.

WORDS TO KNOW

carnivore: an animal that eats other animals.

omnivore: an animal that eats both animals and plants.

revered: to respect and worship.

tattoo: a permanent picture or design marked on the skin.

rabies: a fatal disease transmitted by the saliva of infected animals.

—FASCINATING FACT—

The glass frog is completely transparent except for its intestines, green bones, and beating heart.

Mosquitoes and Insects: Believe it or not, the most dangerous predators in the Amazon are the ones you can barely see—insects. More than 90 percent of the animal species in the Amazon are insects. And a single square mile of rainforest is home to more than 50,000 insect species.

The most dangerous insects aren't those that are poisonous or bite really hard (although those can hurt). No, the most dangerous are the ones that carry disease. Disease-carrying mosquitoes and other insects kill more people in Amazonia than all other kinds of predators combined.

Most of the diseases carried by insects in the Amazon are parasites. Parasites travel through blood and saliva. For example, if an insect bites someone who is infected with a parasite, that parasite gets into the insect. So when that insect bites its next victim, it transfers the parasite through its saliva into that person's bloodstream, spreading the disease.

Malaria

One of the most common—and dangerous—diseases carried by mosquitoes is **malaria**. Malaria is a serious and sometimes fatal blood disease caused by parasites. After entering the body, the parasites multiply quickly in red blood cells. Symptoms of malaria are recurring chills, fever, jaundice, and anemia. Jaundice is a condition where your skin turns yellow.

For centuries, Native Amazonians boiled the bark of the cinchona tree to treat malaria. The boiling produced a substance we call **quinine**. Today there are several different kinds of drugs used to treat malaria. But the best thing is to avoid being bitten in the first place. You need to use a mosquito net when you are sleeping in the rainforest. You should also wear long-sleeved shirts and pants while you're in the rainforest. There isn't a vaccine for malaria, but there are drugs you can take if you plan to go to areas where malaria is common.

—FASCINATING FACT—

The top five predators in the Amazon rainforest (beside insects) are the jaguar, giant otter, black caiman, harpy eagle, and anaconda.

The Incredibly Repulsive Botfly

The botfly won't kill you—but it will completely disgust you. This common hairy fly lays its eggs on mosquitoes. When a mosquito bites you, the botfly egg hatches and the **larva** burrows into your skin. At first it will seem like you have a mildly infected mosquito bite. But as the botfly larva grows under your skin, a painful lump starts to grow. The lump will have a small pinhole in it that the larva breathes through. What's happening is that the larva is growing bigger, and it's eating you, underneath your skin.

Removing botfly larva is tricky because the larva anchors itself under your skin. The most common way to remove a larva is to plug up the breathing hole with petroleum jelly or duct tape. This makes the larva come closer to the surface to get air. Then it can usually be pulled or squeezed out. Sometimes, though, the larva has to be surgically removed. After the larva has been pulled out, it leaves a big hole in your skin.

WORDS TO KNOW

malaria: a blood disease caused by parasites often found in jungle and rainforest environments. It is spread by mosquitoes.

quinine: a bitter-tasting drug made from cinchona tree bark that is used to treat malaria.

larva: the young form of an insect, much like an insect baby.

LOCATION IS IMPORTANT

When you're in the rainforest, you can't start thinking about shelter just as it's getting dark. That's too late. You need to have enough time to scout out a good location and get whatever supplies you need. You have to start planning your shelter during the day.

Where you build your shelter is very important. The location should be close to drinking water, but never near creeks, swamps, and riverbanks, especially during the rainy season, which is November to March. Even dry creek beds can flood incredibly quickly. All it takes is one night of heavy rain.

Many travelers find this out the hard way. For example, a Brazilian outdoorsman with lots of experience planned to spend the night in the rainforest with his wife. They hung their hammocks, one above the other, from a tree next to a very small creek. They figured they would be safe there. The creek was tiny, and their hammocks were tied pretty high in the tree.

They were wrong. It rained all night and the man's wife woke him up to tell him that she was lying in water. He turned on his flashlight and saw that they were completely surrounded by a lake of floodwaters. His wife climbed up into his hammock, and they stayed there for the night. The next day the floodwaters receded and they got safely back on dry land.

FASCINATING FACT

Rivers in the Amazon can flood up to 60 feet (18 meters) during the rainy season. When you look for a good place to camp, check for tell-tale signs of flooding. These include watermarks on tree trunks and brush and debris in tree branches.

A shelter under large trees with lots of dead branches can also be dangerous. Believe it or not, most accidents in the rainforest don't involve animals, but falling trees and branches! Many trees aren't rooted very strongly because the soil is so poor and full of water. Strong storms and gusty winds can push rainforest trees over much more easily than trees in other parts of the world.

Follow the Three S's

If you ever meet an animal in the rainforest, try to follow the three S's.

No sound: be as quiet as possible.

No smell: keep your clothes as clean as possible.

No speed: stay as still as possible. Most animals will not attack you unless they feel threatened. They would much rather run than fight. Wouldn't you?

Falling fruit is also a danger. Palm and nut trees have large, hard fruit that can fall quickly. Brazil nuts, for example, have shells that weigh more than four pounds. Getting hit on the head by a Brazil nut could knock you unconscious. So you would want to look up before you choose your camping place.

BUILDING A SHELTER

Finding a safe place for a shelter in the rainforest is just the first step in spending the night there. Then you need to clear away any old leaves and branches on the ground. Snakes, spiders, biting ants, and other insects live in the brush. Use a stick—not your hands!—to clear away brush, leaves, and branches. After all, the best spots to camp are also the best places to live if you're a snake.

It's also a good idea to dig a trench around your shelter, especially in the wet season. Try to dig it about 6 inches (15 centimeters) deep and at least 7 inches (18 centimeters) wide. This trench will act as a water drain if it rains hard during the night.

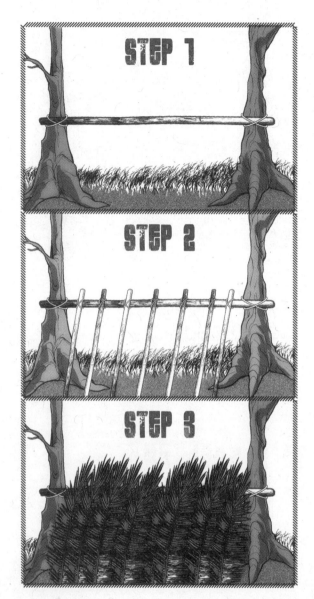

The simplest shelter to build is a lean-to. This is a shelter that has one sloping roof. You can build it with only a knife, a few logs or sticks, a long length of thin liana, and lots of palm fronds. There is liana everywhere in the rainforest. It makes a great, flexible rope. Palm fronds are also very easy to find. You can pick them from low trees or even just find them lying on the ground. Remember that if you take anything off the forest floor, touch it first with a stick, not your hands. Check it carefully before you pick it up.

To build your shelter, you need to find two trees about 6 feet (2 meters) apart. You'll also need a thick stick about 8 feet (2½ meters) long. This will be your roof pole. Now you just need six or seven sticks about 6 feet (2 meters) long.

First, tie each end of the roof pole to the trees with pieces of liana (use the timber hitch—see next page). You should tie them around chest-high. Then lean the other sticks against the roof pole so you have the beginnings of a wall on one side. Make sure the sticks are long and thick enough so they won't collapse. Tie the top of each stick to the roof pole with liana. Then take the palm fronds and lay them lengthwise against these sticks. Eventually you should have a solid wall that will protect you from large animals and bad weather.

TRY THIS: tie simple knots

Even if you don't have to build a shelter in the rainforest, learning how to tie some basic knots will always come in handy. Here's how to tie two knots that are great for building shelters. These are called the Two Half-Hitch and the Timber Hitch.

TWO HALF-HITCH:

The two-half hitch can hold a reasonable load and is easy to loosen.
1. Hook your rope around a post or tree.
2. Cross the short end under the long, main part of the rope.
3. Bring the short end over and down through the hole between where the rope crosses and the pole.
4. Push the knot to the pole and pull to tighten.

You've just made a half hitch. To make a two half hitch, repeat steps 1 through 4, placing the second half hitch beyond the first one.

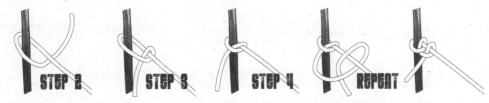

TIMBER HITCH:

The timber half hitch is really useful for tying a rope around a pole or group of logs. The harder you pull it, the more it tightens. It is really easy to loosen.
1. Hook your rope around a post or tree. Leave a long end on one side.
2. Cross the long end over the shorter end.
3. Tuck the long end under itself, working back around the post. Do this multiple times, weaving the long end around the rope that is around the post, until you run out of rope. Your rope will look a bit like a braid.
4. Pull hard on the rope to tighten it.

STEP 2   STEP 3   REPEAT STEP 3   REPEAT STEP 3   STEP 4

Animal Eyeshine

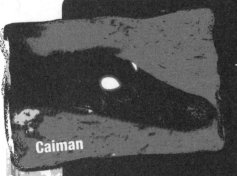

Caiman

The eyes of many nocturnal animals are designed for night vision. Unlike humans, nocturnal animals have a mirror-like layer of tissue inside their eyes that reflects light. This makes things seem brighter. And it's why some animal's eyes seem to shine in the dark. The name for this is eyeshine.

Different animals have different colored eyeshine. You can even tell different species of Amazonian caimans by their eyeshine. The eyes of spectacled caimans look yellow. The eyes of dwarf forest caimans are orange. Black caimans, the largest of the freshwater crocodiles, have eyes that glow ruby red when they are caught by the light of a flashlight. If you are out on the water at night and see ruby red eyes staring back at you, remember that black caimans can grow as long as 20 feet (6 meters) and have been known to eat people.

TRY THIS: Deciphering Animal Tracks

You can find animal tracks almost anywhere. The most common animal tracks belong to birds, dogs, cats, deer, and rodents. Cat and dog tracks look very similar—they both have four toes and a center pad. But cat tracks do not show nail marks. If you see nail marks above the toes, then the prints belong to a dog.

If you find a print that looks like a dog but has five toes, that's a raccoon print. Raccoon toe prints are also usually much thinner. Sometimes you'll even see the brush marks from a raccoon's tail mixed in with the paw prints.

Bird prints are easy: they look like tripod marks. They have three toes fanning out from the joint. The larger or deeper the mark, the bigger the bird. Deer tracks are also easy. They have cloven hooves, which are hooves split in two. So their tracks look a bit like a heart stamped into the mud or snow.

Squirrels and chipmunks make tracks that are clustered together in widely separated groups. That's because they are bounding animals. They have long bodies that spring forward so all four feet land close together. Squirrel marks are usually larger than chipmunk marks.

USING NATURAL SHELTER

Sometimes you can find natural shelter, such as a cave or rock outcropping. But you would want to carefully check for other creatures that could be dangerous. For example, caves are usually home to bats. Use your nose to check for guano—bat droppings—which tells you if the cave is occupied by night fliers. Remember that while most bats are fruit and insect eaters, vampire bats will see you as a convenient snack. Also remember that damp, dark places are ideal homes for snakes, spiders, and other insects.

USING EXISTING SHELTER

It's possible to find man-made shelters in the rainforest. Some of these may have been built by Native Amazonians. Some may have been built by settlers, miners, trappers, fishermen, or loggers. These people often use shelters on and off throughout the year. If you find a man-made shelter you're in luck! Look for signs of recent use, such as supplies or the remains of a fire—you may meet up with another traveler in the rainforest.

An old or unused shelter has probably been abandoned. Be careful using abandoned shelters. It's important to brush out any debris and check all corners. Look out for spiders, especially the super-aggressive banana spider. If you don't, you could end up like John Walden.

Walden, a veteran of more than 75 Amazon expeditions, once made camp in an abandoned shelter in Venezuela. He put up his hammock in the shelter, but didn't sweep away the debris underneath. During the night John got up to go to the bathroom. He reached down and pulled on his boots without shaking them out first. A banana spider that had been lurking in the debris under his hammock had crawled inside one of the boots. It bit him twice on the foot. For more than eight hours, John was in excruciating pain. His foot swelled enormously, and he had a strange sense of being paralyzed. Luckily for him, banana spider bites are usually not fatal. After a day or so he was back to normal.

Beware the Banana Spider

The banana spider looks like a huge tarantula. It can have a leg span of up to 5 inches (13 centimeters) wide, and its fangs are a quarter of an inch long. But unlike the tarantula, which is really harmless, the banana spider is both aggressive and poisonous. Its poison is related to the same poison carried by the black widow spider. The banana spider's latin name is *Phoneutria nigraventer*, meaning "fierce killer." It can also jump as far as 3 feet (1 meter) in one leap.

When the banana spider is ready to attack, it leans back on its hind legs and raises its front ones, cocking itself like the hammer of a gun. The banana spider's bite isn't usually fatal, but it is always incredibly painful. The banana spider is also sometimes called the wandering spider. This is because it travels on the jungle floor and finds shelter in different places rather than building a nest in one location. So you have to be on the lookout for the banana spider any time you are looking for shelter in the rainforest.

MAKE A SLEEPING PLATFORM

Sleeping on the bare ground in this part of the world is definitely a bad idea. Most people use a hammock, a tarp, and mosquito netting to keep them safe, dry, and protected. It's also easy to build a small sleeping platform.

The easiest sleeping platform to make is similar to a raft. In the rainforest you would use bamboo and liana but any wood and twine will work. Cut pieces of bamboo three to 4 feet (1 meter) long. Then notch a window on opposite ends of each section near the end. Lay each bamboo piece on the ground one after another until you have a platform long enough for your body. Line up the windows in each piece of bamboo and run a stick lengthwise through them. Then tie the pieces together with liana. This will make a fairly sturdy sleeping platform that you can adjust to make longer or shorter. This sleeping platform won't keep the mosquitoes off, but it will help keep you dry by holding you up off the damp ground.

BUILDING A FIRE

The best way to keep nighttime insects and other predators away is to build a smoky fire. Building a fire in the Amazon rainforest can be tricky because the constant humidity makes it difficult to find dry wood, even in the dry season. The trees also have less resin than trees in other climates (pine trees in North America, for example, have lots of resin). That means the trees in the Amazon don't burn as quickly or as hot.

Native Amazonians have several methods for starting fires, most of which use friction. Members of the Tirio tribe in Guyana rub together the dead stems of the "ah-de-gah-nah-mah" bush, which is a close relative of the chocolate tree. Other Native Amazonians start fires using bamboo fire saws.

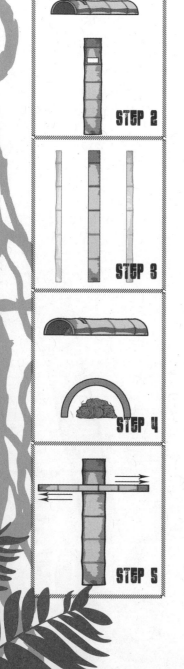

STEP 1

STEP 2

STEP 3

STEP 4

STEP 5

Bamboo fire saws are a little complicated to make and it still takes a lot of work to get the fire going. But a fire is welcome at night in the rainforest.

To make a bamboo fire saw, you'll need to cut a thick piece of bamboo (2 to 3 inches or 5 to 8 centimeters wide) into a section about 2 feet (less than 1 meter) long. Then split the bamboo piece down the middle. Lay one piece flat on the ground, hollow side down. Use a knife to cut a groove lengthwise down the middle.

Now you need to find some tinder. The lighter and fluffier it is, the better. For example, you can shave pieces of the inside part of the bamboo stick into light fluff. Put a little ball of fluff underneath the hollow bamboo, right under the groove. Now take the other piece of the bamboo. Cut away the rounded edges until the bamboo piece is more straight than rounded. It should look a bit like a violin bow. This is your saw.

Now put your knee on the piece of bamboo on the ground to hold it still. Then very quickly move the saw back and forth across the groove. This creates friction, and friction creates heat. Eventually the grooved area of the bamboo should start to smoke and sparks will drop down onto the fluff underneath. As soon as you see sparks, stop sawing and quickly lift up the bamboo. Start blowing gently on the fluff to keep the tiny fire going. Then put the burning fluff into more tinder, and use this to build a fire.

This isn't easy, and chances are you'll accidentally blow out any sparks you make the first few times. But if you have patience and energy, a bamboo fire saw is the best way to make a fire in the rainforest if you don't have matches.

Nighttime fires are also good for keeping insects away. The smokier the fire, the better. The very best fuel for a smoky fire in the Amazon rainforest is termite nests. They give off a smoke that mosquitoes can't stand. In fact, many native Amazonian tribes rub burnt termite nest on their faces and bodies when they go into the forest. Then the insects don't bother them at all.

Scientists have recently discovered why termite nests work so well as insect repellent. The nests are full of a chemical called naphthalene, which is a natural insecticide. You probably know what naphthalene smells like—it is a main ingredient in mothballs. People put mothballs in their closets to keep their wool clothes from being eaten by moths.

TRY THIS: Light a Fire Without Matches

If you have sunlight and a magnifying glass, a pair of eyeglasses, or even a clear bottle, you can start a fire without matches. Gather some light, fluffy tinder and put it on a slightly raised surface, such as a pile of sticks. You need air both underneath and on top of the tinder. Then hold the magnifying glass and focus a pinpoint of bright light directly on the tinder. Hold it there long enough and you'll see smoke start to rise. Blow very gently from below to help feed the flame.

END NOTE 1

Supplies for an Amazon Adventure

If you had the chance to take an Amazonian adventure you'd need to be well prepared. Here's a list of basic supplies for exploring the Amazon.

On Your Feet

Boots or trail shoes that you can wear in mud, water, and walking over rocks. They should have a good tread and nylon uppers so they dry fast. Your feet are bound to get wet when you're in the rainforest, so quick-drying material is important. Over-the-ankle shoes give you a little more protection from snakes and other creatures.

Rubber boots with a good sole for wearing around camp. These will help keep your feet dry when you aren't on the trail. Remember to always shake out your boots and shoes before putting them on!

Supplies for an Amazon Adventure

Lightweight socks, but not cotton. Cotton won't dry quickly in the humidity of the rainforest.

Don't go barefoot, and don't wear open-toed sandals in the rainforest. You've learned enough about the plants and animals of Amazonia to know that covering your feet is really important.

On Your Body

Lightweight, long-sleeved shirts and long pants. You may be fine with a short-sleeved shirt during the day, but you'll probably want something with more protection from insects at night.

A sweater or sweatshirt made of a lightweight but breathable fabric. Don't wear cotton sweatshirts or denim jeans. They will get wet and heavy and won't dry properly in the humidity of the rainforest. Stick with quick-dry fabrics.

A hat and a waterproof rain jacket. These are vital. A hat is great for keeping you cool—and for making sure creepy crawlies don't land on your head. And remember that parts of Amazonia can receive up to 6½ *feet* (2 meters) of rain a year. It's going to rain while you are there. Don't spend your trip being miserable because you forgot a rain jacket.

For Sleeping

A hammock. These are portable, lightweight, and easy to put up almost anywhere.

A mosquito net. These are designed to fit over hammocks and can save you a sleepless night. It will also help protect you from all kinds of night-flying insects.

For Eating and Drinking

A plastic water bottle is rugged and won't retain odors. Include a clip or carabineer so you can clip it to your pack or belt.

Iodine tablets to help purify water. You've learned about some of the water-borne diseases of Amazonia, and don't want to risk getting any.

A knife and spoon.

A fishing line and several fishhooks. You might want to make your own (see chapter 4), but you'll have an easier time catching fish with a steel hook rather than one made from thorns.

A multi-tool or Swiss Army Knife that has a sawing blade on it, and a machete. Both will come in really handy for everything from gutting fish to cutting out palm hearts to digging for palm grubs.

Other Gear

A backpack and a smaller daypack. The backpack can hold most of your gear, and the daypack will let you take just what you need for smaller, day trips. Try to get the most water-repellent kind of fabric on your packs as possible.

Waterproof matches or a butane lighter. It's also a really good idea to bring a small supply of very small, shredded tire strips with you as tinder. You can definitely try making a fire with a bamboo fire saw, or even bring flint and steel, but the most foolproof method for starting a fire in the damp rainforest is by using a lighter and thin strips of old tires.

Insect repellent—or find a termite nest that you can burn and rub on you. If you use insect repellent with DEET, make sure it has less than 30 percent. Anything containing more than 30 percent DEET is a real health hazard to you.

A whistle. You may never need it, but if you happen to get separated from your family, friends, or fellow campers, having a whistle and an agreed-upon signal for "help! I'm lost!" can mean the difference between a quick scare and a real disaster.

END NOTE 2

Help Save the Amazon Rainforest!

The Amazon Rainforest needs your help! More than 20 percent of the rainforest in Amazonia has been destroyed. An average of 80 acres is deforested every day—that's about the size of 14 football fields. Some environmentalists predict that all of Amazonia's rainforests could be gone by 2050.

There is no one group of people to blame for the destruction of the Amazon rainforest. It's a very complicated issue. But you can be a part of the solution. Even though you're "just a kid," here are some ways you can help save Amazonia's plants, animals, and people for future generations of kids just like you.

Recycle! Much of the Amazon's forests are logged to make paper! By using recycled paper products you are helping to save some of the Amazon's forests. So reduce, reuse, and recycle as much as you can—and buy recycled products whenever possible.

Buy locally-bred pets. If you buy pets like tropical fish, snakes, or reptiles, make sure you buy animals that have been bred in captivity. Lots of Amazonian animals, including tropical fish, are becoming endangered because of overhunting. Make sure the exotic pets you buy were not caught in the wild.

Become an activist. Join environmental groups that support Amazon conservation (see the list of Resources for good websites for this). Learn about the companies that you buy products from. Find out if they buy their materials from the Amazon rainforest. Support companies that have a strong commitment to the environment. You may like the products a company makes, but if they are hurting the rainforest, then so are you.

Get educated. Read about what is happening in Amazonia and why the rainforest is becoming deforested so quickly. You can read newspapers or get updates on the web. Understand the problem.

Talk about it! Talk about the importance of saving the natural resources of the Amazon with your parents, your teachers, and your friends. Encourage the adults in your life to get involved!

You can be part of the solution! Get active!

BIBLIOGRAPHY

Online News Stories/Sources

"Amazon Rainforest Greens Up in the Dry Season." *Science Daily*.
www.sciencedaily.com. 23 March 2006.

"Sahara Dust: Savior of the Amazon Rainforest?" *World Climate Report*,
worldclimatereport.com. 9 March 2007.

"Source of the Amazon River," *Earth Observatory News*.
Earthobservatory.nasa.gov. 2007.

Bonsor, Kevin. "How Quicksand Works." *How Stuff Works*,
www.howstuffworks.com.

Butler, Rhett A. "The Amazon: The World's Largest Rainforest." Mongabay.com/
A Place Out of Time: Tropical Rainforests and the Perils They Face.
6 January 2008.

Kornreich, David. "Why Is Twilight Short Near the Equator?" *Curious About
Astronomy*, Cornell University, www.curious.astro.cornell.edu.

Miller, Carolyn. "Measurement of Jaguar Tracks: a promising means to identify
individuals." Wildlife Conservation Society. www.savethejaguar.com. July 2001.

Roach, John. "Amazon Longer Than Nile River, Scientists Say."
National Geographic News, www.nationalgeographic.com. 18 June 2007.

Roach, John. "Amazon Tribes Isolated By Choice?" *National Geographic News*,
www.nationalgeographic.com. 10 March 2003.

Rodrigues, Mabel. "South American Poisonous Frog." *Ask a Scientist Zoology
Archive*. www.newton.dep.anl.gov/askasci/zoo00/zoo00593.htm

BIBLIOGRAPHY

Websites

www.amazonia.org
www.amazon-indians.org
www.amazon-rainforest.org
www.amazonswim.com
www.amazonteam.org
www.extremescience.com/AmazonRiver.html
www.mongabay.com
www.nationalgeographic.com/wildworld.html
www.pbs.org/journeyintoamazonia
www.nationalgeographic.com/wildworld.html
www.rainforestweb.org
www.safegardening.co.uk/ediblewildplants.html

Magazines/Reports

"Brief History and Introduction of Rubber." International Institute of Synthetic Rubber Producers, Incl. www.iisrp.com/WebPolymers/00Rubber_Intro.pdf

Chmielinksi, Piotr. "Kayaking the Amazon." *National Geographic*, Vol 171, No. 4, April 1987.

Gonzales, Laurence. "Why Smart People Make Dumb Mistakes (And How You Can Avoid Them)," *National Geographic Adventure*, August 2007, pp 45-51.

Howells, Robert Earl. "The Adventurer's Handbook: 30 Crucial Skills, Nifty Tips, and Shameless Shortcuts." *National Geographic Adventure*, January/February 2002.

Koren, I., Y.J. Kaufman, R. Washington, M.C. Todd, Y. Rudich, J.V. Martins and D. Rosenfeld, 2006. The Bodélé depression: a single spot in the Sahara that provides most of the mineral dust to the Amazon Forest. *Environmental Research Letters*, 1, doi: 10.1088/1748-9326/1/1014005.

BIBLIOGRAPHY

Martin, Stella. "Eyeshine." *Tropical Topics*. Publication of Environmental Protection Agency, Queensland, Australia. No.48, July 1998.

Steadman, John. "How to Fillet a Fish." *Popular Mechanic*s, October 2007.

Von Puttkamer, W. Jesco. "Brazil Protects Her Cinta Largas," *National Geographic*, September 1971.

Wallace, Scott. "Last of the Amazon." *National Geographic*, Vol.211, No.4, January 2007, pp 40–71.

Books

Bell, Biran, and Maria Lord, Eds. *Amazon Wildlife*. Insight Guide. London: Langenscheidt, 2002.

Cherrie, George. Dark Trails; *Adventures of a Naturalist*. New York: G. P. Putnam's sons, 1930.

Coningham, John. *Walking the Jungle: An Adventurer's Guide to the Amazon*. Short Hills, NJ: Burford Books, 2003.

Cousteau, Jacques-Yves, and Mose Richards. *Jacques Cousteau's Amazon Journey*. New York: Harry N. Abrams, 1984.

Davis, Wade. *One River: Explorations and Discoveries in the Amazon Rain Forest*. New York: Simon & Schuster, 1996.

Dorson, Mercedes, and Jeanne Wilmot. *Tales from the Amazon Rain Forest*. Hopewell, New Jersey: Ecco Press, 1997.

Gatty, Harold. *Finding Your Way Without a Map or Compass*. Mineola, New York: Dover Publications, 1983.

Ghinsberg, Yossi. *Back from Tuichi: The Harrowing Life-And-Death Story of Survival in the Amazon Rainforest*. New York: Random House, 1993.

Goulding, Michael. *The Fishes and the Forest: Explorations in Amazonian Natural History*. Berkeley: University of California Press, 1980.

BIBLIOGRAPHY

Books continued

Millard, Candice. *The River of Doubt: Theodore Roosevelt's Darkest Journey.* New York: Random House, 2005.

Montgomery, Sy. *Journey of the Pink Dolphins: An Amazon Quest.* New York: Simon & Schuster, 2000.

Plotkin, Mark J, Ph.D. *Tales of a Shaman's Apprentice: An Ethnobotanist Searches for New Medicines in the Amazon Rainforest.* New York: Penguin, 1983.

Rondon, Colonel Candido Mariano da Silva. *Lectures delivered by Colonel Candido Mariano da Silva Rondon, Chief of the Commission, on the 5th, 7th, and 9th of October, 1915, at the Phennix Theatre of Rio de Janeiro, on the Roosevelt-Rondon Scientific Expedition and the Telegraph Line Commission.* Translated by R. G. Reidy and Ed. Murray. New York: Greenwood Press, 1969.

Roosevelt, Theodore. *Through the Brazilian Wilderness.* New York: Charles Scribner's Sons, 1914.

Schreider, Helen, and Frank Schreider. *Exploring the Amazon.* Washington, D.C.: The National Geographic Society, 1970.

Schultes, Richard Evans, and Robert F Raffauf. *The Healing Forest: Medicinal and Toxis Plants of the Northwest Amazonia.* Portland, Oregon: Dioscorides Press, 1990.

Shoumatoff, Alex. *The Rivers Amazon.* San Francisco: Sierra Club Books, 1978.

Walden, John. *Jungle Travel & Survival.* Guilford, CT: The Lyons Press, 2001.

RESOURCES

Books

About Rainforests and Amazonia

Albert, Toni. *The Remarkable Rainforest: An Active-Learning Book for Kids.* Trickle Creek Books, 2003.

George, Jean Craighead. *One Day in the Tropical Rainforest.* New York: Harper Trophy, 1995.

Knight, Tim. *Journey into the Rainforest.* Oxford University Press, 2002.

Montgomery, Sy. *Encantado, Pink Dolphin of the Amazon River.* New York: Houghton Mifflin, 2002.

Osborne, Will and Osborne, Mary. *Rainforests (Magic Treehouse Research Guide).* New York: Random House Books for Young Readers, 2001.

Pratt, Kristin Joy. *A Walk in the Rainforest.* Dawn Publication, 1992.

Ryan, Marla, and Elaine Pasco, Eds. *The Jeff Corwin Experience: Into Wild Amazonia.* Black Birch Press, 2004.

About Survival

Brown, Tom. *Tom Brown's Field Guide to Nature and Survival for Children.* Berkeley Publishing, 1989.

Gibbs, Lynn. *What if? A Kid's Guide to Surviving Just About Anything.* Gingham Dog Press, 2002.

Llewellyn, Claire. *Kid's Survival Handbook.* New York: Scholastic, 2002.

Logue, Victoria. *Kids Outdoors: Skills and Knowledge for Outdoor Adventures.* Ragged Mountain Press, 1996.

Whitefeather, Willy. *Willy Whitefeather's Outdoor Survival Handbook for Kids.* Roberts Rhinehart Publishers, 1997.

Television Shows

"Man Vs. Wild," Discovery Channel
"Rick Mears Extreme Survival," BBC
"Survivorman," Discovery Channel

Websites

www.amazonteam.org
www.amazonia.org
www.amazon-indians.org
www.amazon-rainforest.org
www.mongabay.com

www.nationalgeographic.com/wildworld.html
www.pbs.org/journeyintoamazonia
www.rainforestweb.org
www.rain-tree.com

GLOSSARY

alkaloids: natural chemicals found in plants. Nicotine is an alkaloid.

Amazonia: a huge area surrounding the Amazon river in northern South America.

Amazons: a nation of fierce, women warriors in Greek mythology.

amoeba: a single-celled organism found in water. It is a parasite.

amphibians: animals like frogs, toads, and salamanders. The young have gills like fish but adults breathe air.

anaconda: large constrictor of tropical South America, usually living in swamps or slow-moving water.

Andes Mountains: one of the longest and highest mountain ranges in the world. The Andes run 4,500 miles (7,242 kilometers) along the west coast of South America.

atmosphere: the air or gas surrounding a planet.

bacteria: microorganisms found in soil, water, plants, and animals that are sometimes harmful.

balsa: a tropical tree with very light wood that floats.

bamboo: a type of tropical grass that resembles a tree. Its wood is hollow and solid and it can grow extremely quickly, up to a couple of feet per day!

blaze: to mark out a path or trail.

blowgun: a tube through which darts can be shot. It is held to the mouth like a straw and is used today by some Native Amazonians to hunt prey.

bromeliads: a tropical plant family that includes the pineapple.

buoyancy: the force that makes something able to float.

caiman: a reptile that's very similar to an alligator. It lives in Central and South America.

cairn: a mound of stones piled on top of each other to mark a path.

carnivore: an animal that eats other animals.

carnivorous: a plant or animal that eats meat. Some plants trap and digest small animals, mostly insects.

catfish: bottom-living fish found in freshwater in the Americas, Europe, and Asia. They usually have "whiskers" around their mouths.

constrictors: a variety of snake that has strong muscles and uses them to squeeze their prey to death.

contaminate: to pollute or make dirty, so the water isn't healthy to drink.

curare: poison made from plant or animal venom, used for hunting.

decay: the process of rotting or deteriorating.

dehydrated: suffering from a great loss of water in the body.

diurnal: active during the day.

diverse: lots of different species.

downstream: in the direction of a stream's current, away from its source.

ecosystem: a community of animals and plants existing and interacting together.

eel: a fish that is long and snake-like.

epiphytes: plants that grow on other plants. They get their food and water from the air and rain.

equator: an invisible circle around the earth halfway between the North and South Poles.

GLOSSARY

floodplain: a flat, low area next to a river. The river often floods the flood plain, providing nutrients that help plants grow.

forage: search for food.

fungus: a plant-like organism without leaves or flowers that grows on other plants or decaying material. Examples are mold, mildew, and mushrooms.

habitat: an area where a species or groups of different animals and plants live.

hectare: a metric unit of land equal to 107,000 square feet, or about 2½ acres.

humid: a high level of moisture in the air.

ice ages: periods in time when the earth cools down and ice spreads over a large part of the planet.

immunity: when a person has been exposed to a disease before and can resist it.

infest: to live in or on in great numbers as a parasite.

insecticide: a chemical that kills insects.

kayak: a light, narrow canoe useful for traveling in fast currents.

landmark: a noticeable natural or man-made feature used for navigation.

larva: the young form of an insect, much like an insect baby.

latex: a product of rubber trees from which rubber can be made.

leech: a wormlike animal found in water that latches on to another animal's skin and sucks its blood.

lianas: long, woody vines found in the Amazon and other areas of the world as well.

lichen: a plant-like organism made of algae and fungus that grows on solid surfaces such as rocks or trees.

lowlands: land that is lower and flatter than surrounding lands.

lush: word to describe lots of richly green plants.

malaria: a blood disease caused by parasites often found in jungle and rainforest environments. It is spread by mosquitoes.

malnourished: when you don't get enough of the right food to keep you healthy and strong.

mammals: a class of animals that includes humans. These animals have backbones, nourish their young with milk, and are mostly covered with hair.

manatee: a large, plant-eating mammal that lives and swims in the Amazon and other parts of the world, including India and Florida.

medicinal: having properties that can be used to treat illness.

microhabitat: a very small, specialized habitat. This can even be a clump of grass or a space between rocks.

mildew: a fungus that often looks white and can be found on rotting food and plants.

minerals: nutrients found in rocks and soil that keep plants and animals healthy and growing.

mosquito net: a net that does not allow mosquitoes to get through. It can be draped over a bed or a sleeping area to protect you in the night.

Nile River: a long river in Africa (4,132 miles or 6,650 kilometers) that winds its way from Burundi to Egypt.

nocturnal: nocturnal animals are active at night.

Northern Hemisphere: the half of the earth that is north of the equator. This includes North America, Europe, Asia, the Middle East, and Northern Africa.

GLOSSARY

nutrients: the substances in food and soil that keep animals and plants healthy and growing.

omnivore: an animal that eats both animals and plants.

orchids: rare and beautiful flowers.

organs: things like the heart, lungs, stomach, and liver.

palm: a tropical tree with fronds.

parasite: an animal or plant that lives on or in another plant or animal, feeding off of it, without any benefit to the host.

perpendicular: when an object forms a right angle with another object.

predator: an animal that eats other animals.

prey: an animal hunted by a predator.

propagate: create new plants.

property: a quality or feature of something; the way something is.

quinine: a bitter-tasting drug made from cinchona tree bark that is used to treat malaria.

rabies: a fatal disease transmitted by the saliva of infected animals.

rainforest: a forest in a hot climate that gets a lot of rain every year, so the plants are very green and grow like crazy.

resin: a substance from plants that is sticky like glue.

revered: to respect and worship.

rubber: a material made from latex, which is found in rubber trees in the Amazon.

Sahara Desert: the world's largest desert, located in northern Africa.

salicylic acid: an acid from a willow tree that is used to make aspirin.

sapling: a young tree.

savannah: a large grassy area with few trees.

shaman: a native person with the power to heal.

silt: soil made up of fine bits of rock. This soil is often left on land when floods recede.

species: a group of plants or animals that are closely related and look the same.

stagnant: very still, not moving.

stillwater lake: a lake within the boundaries of a wetland, often surrounded by swamp-like plants and habitat.

stingray: an animal, found in the water. It is flat and has a long tail with sharp barbs on the end. It likes to hide beneath the mud, and its barbed tail can really hurt passing fish (or people!)

symmetrical: the same on both sides.

tannins: substances found in plants that are used to turn animal skins into leather.

tattoo: a permanent picture or design marked on the skin.

toxic: poisonous.

tributary: a river or stream that flows into a larger lake or river.

tropical: a hot climate, usually near the equator.

upstream: against the direction of a stream's current, toward its source.

vipers: a venomous variety of snake that is poisonous.

watershed: an area where all the water drains into one river or lake.

Western Hemisphere: the half of the earth that contains North and South America.

wetland: a low-lying area that is filled with water.

Index

Index

M

malaria, 44, 64
manatees, 37
map, 4
medicines, 44, 64
monkeys, 12, 44
mosquitoes, 64–65
Mount Mismi, 7–8

N

native Amazonians
    ceremonies of, 23, 62
    diseases and, 13, 44, 55, 63–64
    fire starting by, 73
    food and, 40, 45–46, 50
    insecticides and, 75
    population of, 13–14
    travel in Amazonia and, 16, 19
Nile River, 8
nocturnal animals, 61–63, 70
noises/sounds, 5, 43–44, 61, 67
nomads, 39, 41
nutrients, 29, 31, 39, 40.
    See also food

P

palm grubs, 46
palm trees, 17, 39, 45–46, 67–68
parasites, 35, 48, 53–54, 64
parrots, 57
peccaries, 43–44
people. *See* native Amazonians
Peru, 4, 7–8, 16
piranha, 37
plants. *See also* trees
    defense mechanisms of, 23–24,
        57
    as food, 38–46
    for shelters, 68, 73
    travel in Amazonia and, 18–19,
        23–24, 31–32
    typical, in rainforest, 5, 9–11,
        13, 16
    as water source, 53, 56–57
poison, 20, 41–43, 46, 47, 50, 57,
    61, 72

poison dart frogs, 47, 61
population, 14
predators/prey, 16, 20, 24, 30, 33,
    35–37, 43–44, 47, 61–64

Q

quicksand, 33–34
quinine, 44, 64

R

rafting/rafts, 28, 32, 34
rainforest. *See also* plants; trees
    definition of, 3
    description of, 5, 9–13
    flooding in, 31–32, 66
    nighttime in, 60–75
    protection of, 79–80
    travel through, 15–26
Rio Amazonas, 6–8, 16, 28, 31
Rio Negro, 7, 31
Rio Solimões, 7, 31
rivers, 6–8, 16, 27–37, 56, 66
rotenone, 50
rubber, 14

S

shelters, 60, 66–68, 71–73
ships/boats, 6, 28.
    See also rafting/rafts
shoes/boots, 72, 76
silt, 7
slavery, 13–14
sleeping platforms, 73
snail fever, 54
snakes, 11, 17, 20, 35–36, 59, 67,
    71, 80
sounds/noises, 5, 43–44, 61, 67
South America, 4, 5–7, 9
spiders, 17, 67, 71–72
sun/sunlight, 10–11, 21, 24, 61
swimming, 8, 29, 37, 53–54

T

termite nests, 75
tracks (animal), 70
trail blazing, 18–19
travel
    becoming lost during, 15–16, 22,
        24, 63
    in rainforest, 15–26
    supplies for, 76–78
    by water, 27–37
trees
    defense mechanisms of, 24
    for fires, 73–74
    flooding and, 31–32
    food and, 45–46
    layers of, 10–12
    rubber, 14
    for shelters, 67–68, 73
    travel in Amazonia and, 17–19,
        21, 24, 29, 31–32
    typical, in rainforest, 5, 10–12,
        39
    as water source, 57
tribes. *See* native Amazonians

U

understory layer, 11

V

vampire bats, 63, 71
vines, 10, 13, 23, 32, 56–57, 68, 73

W

water, 7, 27–37, 52–59, 77.
    See also rivers
weapons, 46, 49–50
weather. *See* climate
whitewater rivers, 29, 31
worms, 11, 47